GET READY TO LEARN
SOME ENGLISH!

TAKE IT SLOW & ENJOY
THE JOURNEY!

SUCCESS COMES
WHEN YOU DON'T GIVE
UP!

**77 Real Life English Dialogues -**

**500 Most Common English Words**



Book design & layout by Calvin Hanson Creative

---



Inquiries: hello@learnenglishwithcamille.com

ISBN 9798395099204 (paperback)

Independently Published

First printing 2023

# TABLE OF CO

# How to use this book

I'm so glad you're here! Do you know how many words you need to know to become conversational? Many sources say you need to learn 500 words to become "basic conversational." With that in mind, I wrote this book of 77 Real Life English Dialogues using the top 500 words in American English. I spent hours comparing many lists of words online and then I compiled my own list using those words.

This book is divided into sections, for example, dialogues at work, dialogues at school, dialogues at home, etc. I organized it this way so you see the most common words in the context of everyday dialogues.

This book is accompanied with FREE audio to listen to the dialogues in both slow and normal speed. This book can benefit both the beginner and intermediate English language learner.

At the end of the book you will find an alphabetized list of all the words with their meaning and an example sentence.

You will see the same 500 words used throughout this book. My hope is that you will know how to use the top 500 words in English in context and that this book and audio will help you on your way to fluency.

**Remember to have fun! Thanks for letting me be a part of your English learning journey.**

**FREE AUDIO DOWNLOAD**

Please go to PAGE 39 for link

Note: This protects the audio from the free Amazon preview.

DIALOGUE 1

# Introductions

**Ben:** Hi. How are you?

**Julia:** I'm great, thanks. And you?

**Ben:** Doing well. Meet my wife Sue, our little girl Jill, and her baby brother Ryan.

**Julia:** So nice to meet you all. This is my husband Luca and our wild, yet sweet dog Zippy.

**Ben:** It's so fun to meet you all too. We have never been to this part of the town before.

**Julia:** We love the streets. Let's walk to the center.

**Ben:** Sure, we would love to go eat after. You said there is a lot of good food around here right?

**Julia:** Yes. I think you will be happy with it.

**Ben:** Great. Thanks again for inviting us.

**Julia:** Of course!

DIALOGUE 2

# What is Your Job?

**Sam:** Thanks for meeting me over lunch.

**Alice:** Of course. I actually remember this place. I've been here before.

**Sam:** Wow, cool. What is your job?

**Alice:** I am a history teacher. And what do you do?

**Sam:** I am a student. I'm in college.

**Alice:** That's great. What do you study?

**Sam:** I study science. I want to be a scientist like my father.

**Alice:** That's special. I'm sure he is happy.

**Sam:** I think so. What grade do you teach?

**Alice:** I teach young children. I love that age.

**Sam:** Do you like the school? How long have you taught there?

**Alice:** I do like it. It's nothing like my old school. I've been there for 2 years now.

**Sam:** I'm sure everybody loves you.

**Alice:** I hope so. Do you want to order now?

**Sam:** Yes! I'm so hungry.

DIALOGUE 3

# My Family

**Angel:** Do you have any siblings?

**Jack:** Yes. I have one brother and one sister. You?

**Angel:** No, I'm an only child.

**Jack:** Wow. Were you bored growing up?

**Angel:** No, because my dad has a large family. 5 brothers! I know, a lot of men.

**Jack:** I guess so.

**Angel:** Are you close to both of your siblings?

**Jack:** Yes. My sister lives far away but we often get together. She has a baby girl.

**Angel:** That's good. I'm sure you're the best uncle.

**Jack:** I love to play with her. She makes a lot of funny sounds. She is only one year old.

**Angel:** That age is the best. I have a two, almost three year old cat.

**Jack:** That's nice. I don't have any pets.

**Angel:** They are like babies, little and free.

**Jack:** True, you're right.

DIALOGUE 4

# What does She Look Like?

**Elodie:** You talk a lot about her. What color is her hair?

**Taylor:** She has long black hair and a round face.

**Elodie:** And her eyes?

**Taylor:** They are deep sea green.

**Elodie:** Is she tall or short?

**Taylor:** She is small. Not too tall.

**Elodie:** Really? What's her weight?

**Taylor:** Probably around 120 pounds. She's in good shape.

**Elodie:** It seems like she has a great figure.

**Taylor:** She does. Look at this picture.

**Elodie:** You're right. She's a beauty. I can see why you're interested.

**Taylor:** I'm trying to find the right moment to ask her out.

**Elodie:** Maybe wait a day or two. Follow your heart.

**Taylor:** That's a good idea. I will write her a note or draw her favorite animal.

**Elodie:** Just make sure to spell her name correctly!

**Taylor:** Wish me luck!

**Elodie:** Good luck!

DIALOGUE 5

# What are Your Hobbies?

**Kaylea:** What are your hobbies?

**Matt:** I like to ride my bike and listen to music.

**Kaylea:** I enjoy reading books and traveling.

**Matt:** Oh yes, I want to see the world.

**Kaylea:** Do you speak another language?

**Matt:** I'm trying to learn Portuguese.

**Kaylea**: Is it hard?

**Matt:** I practice every morning during breakfast. It's not so simple.

**Kaylea:** I have never learned another language. I probably should, but I don't know where to start.

**Matt:** You should choose one that interests you.

**Kaylea:** I have a friend who learns every day while she runs.

**Matt:** There are many ways to learn. The point is to do something every day.

**Kaylea:** I wonder how long it will take? One thousand hours?

**Matt:** Probably, but time passes quickly. We only have one life.

**Kaylea:** I will start tomorrow.

**Matt:** Good idea.

DIALOGUE 6

# What's the Weather?

**Jude:** Is it hot or cold today?

**Melodie:** I'm certain it's cold. Look at the mountain. You can see snow on the top.

**Jude:** It is winter. I miss summer and swimming in the river.

**Melodie:** Me too. I miss our boat and the sunshine.

**Jude:** But our house is warm. We have the fire on.

**Melodie:** True. Plus I prefer snow to rain. I love the white sky.

**Jude:** Can I have a group of friends come over this week? We can play in my room or out in the field.

**Melodie:** Sure, that's fine, but you need to make your own food.

**Jude:** I will. Maybe we will play games.

**Melodie:** As long as you remember to finish your school paper first.

**Jude:** I already did.

**Melodie:** Wow. I'm impressed.

**Jude:** Thanks. The bus is here. I have to go now.

**Melodie:** Have a fun day!

**Jude:** You too. Bye.

DIALOGUE 7

# What's your Favorite Season?

**Olivia:** You live on the west coast right?

**Corey:** Yes. Our house is on the sea in southern California.

**Olivia:** Is it hot or cold there? I live on the other side of the country, on the east coast and we have a lot of cold weather.

**Corey:** It's mostly warm, but up in the mountains it can get cooler.

**Olivia:** We have about six months of nice weather here.

**Corey:** Do you prefer summer or winter?

**Olivia:** Actually I prefer both spring and fall because the weather isn't so extreme.

**Corey:** That makes sense. I like summer weather best. We plant a garden every year.

**Olivia:** I would love to grow some herbs this summer.

**Corey:** You should try. You just need to make sure to water them.

**Olivia:** I may need to ask you for help.

**Corey:** I'll be here, call me if you need anything.

**Olivia:** I will.

DIALOGUE 8

# Making Plans

**Luke:** I have a question.

**Lane:** Perhaps I have an answer.

**Luke:** Haha, funny. What's your favorite kind of movie?

**Lane:** I usually watch American films. And you?

**Luke:** I like war movies.

**Lane:** I never watch war movies. I like deep stories, dramas.

**Luke:** I am not against those.

**Lane:** We can watch one together next week. I will be free from 5-8 on Saturday.

**Luke:** Sure. I could come after work. I will be there between 5 and 5:30.

**Lane:** Perfect. Bring some food too.

**Luke:** I just bought some yesterday.

**Lane:** Nice. Since your home is near, will you walk?

**Luke:** It's possible. You're just a few streets away and I need some fresh air.

**Lane:** Text me when you're on your way and I will leave the door open.

**Luke:** I will. Your house is at the end of the road right? The one with the three big green trees in the front?

**Lane:** Exactly. Well, it's all set. I can't wait!

**Luke:** Me neither. See you soon.

DIALOGUE 9

# Real Life Chat

**Melissa:** Do you like to read?

**Travis:** I've been so busy lately that I haven't been reading. But I do like to read.

**Melissa:** Same. It's how I rest.

**Travis:** My schedule has been so full. I'm trying to clear it.

**Melissa**: What if you wake up early?

**Travis:** I would like to, but I'm so tired.

**Melissa:** Have you thought about changing your job?

**Travis**: They said that next month should be better. There is a new person coming from another city to help us.

**Melissa:** Is there room? Your office is not very big.

**Travis:** We will find a place. Something has got to change. I can't do everything myself.

**Melissa:** I agree. Do you feel alone?

**Travis:** A little. It's like I told you before. I must do so many things and I'm tired.

**Melissa:** You need sleep. If you decide to leave your job, I will understand.

**Travis:** I thought about it. However, I want to stay and build this company.

**Melissa:** I know you like being a part of it.

**Travis:** We are a young group and there is a good spirit in the air. We laugh a lot. We just need to work less.

DIALOGUE 10

# My Morning Routine

**Lisa:** Tell me about your morning routine.

**Tom:** I wake up around 6 a.m. I don't use an alarm.

**Lisa:** Your day begins early! Then what do you do?

**Tom:** I wash my face. My wife wakes up at 6:30. I like to have coffee already made for her. I even measure the coffee beans the night before.

**Lisa:** That's nice of you.

**Tom:** Yes. After coffee, I always move my body. Sometimes I bike, sometimes I run.

**Lisa:** Health is important.

**Tom:** It is. Then I lay out my clothes for work and I take a fast shower. I like to be clean.

**Lisa:** Haha, who doesn't?

**Tom:** True. Finally I eat breakfast and talk to my wife. If I have a minute, I read the newspaper.

**Lisa:** Does your wife work?

**Tom:** Yes. She drives to work. We only have one car, so I take the train.

**Lisa:** Do you like to go to work by train?

**Tom:** I like the train more than the car because I can read or work a little.

**Lisa:** You make a good point.

**Tom:** Plus, it doesn't cost much money. On the way home, it's usually dark so I close my eyes and rest my head against the seat.

DIALOGUE 11

# My Bedtime Routine

**Jax:** What do you do every night?

**Kim:** Most nights are the same. I have 4 young children so I have to give them a bath, help them brush their teeth, and put them to bed.

**Jax:** Wow, do they ever fight?

**Kim:** They get along well, but not all the time. If they become overtired, they fight or get mad and cry.

**Jax:** I can imagine.

**Kim:** I am their mother, so I try to set a good example.

**Jax:** You're a great mother.

**Kim:** Thanks. Every night we sing a song or two. We also read stories.

**Jax:** It seems like you found a good routine.

**Kim:** We have. If my husband is back from work, he is able to help me and everything is better.

**Jax:** It helps to have a man to hold things together.

**Kim:** Yes, you never know what might happen with four wild kids.

DIALOGUE 12

# My House

**Katie:** Which house is yours? (on the phone)

**Taylor:** It's the one behind the red one.

**Katie:** Can you stand out front and show me?

**Taylor:** I'm out front now.

**Katie:** Oh, I see you. I came to the wrong house. I'm coming towards you now.

**Taylor:** Pull into the driveway. You can park between the cars or behind the white car.

**Katie:** I'm here! I love this town.

**Taylor:** Us too. We are only a mile from the center.

**Katie:** I feel like I've been to this area before. Maybe once, a long time ago.

**Taylor:** You live an hour south from here, right?

**Katie: Y**es. My husband developed our land and we built a large house.

**Taylor:** That's a slow process, but I'm sure you were happy when it was ready.

**Katie:** Without a doubt. I hope to live there until I die.

**Taylor:** I would love to stop by sometime and see the final product.

**Katie:** You're welcome anytime.

**Taylor:** Thank you!

DIALOGUE 13

# Animals

**Wendy:** You have five birds. That's not very common.

**Dax:** I know, most people have dogs and cats.

**Wendy:** I had a dog when I was a child.

**Dax:** What kind?

**Wendy:** A mastiff, it was as big as a small horse.

**Dax:** Haha, funny. Do you see the blue bird on the left?

**Wendy:** Yes

**Dax:** It's the last one I bought.

**Wendy:** It's still so little. I can't tell if it's trying to sit, stand, or fly away.

**Dax:** Yesterday, I heard a noise, so I went and stood by the cage. Then I saw it was trying to get out.

**Wendy:** What happened?

**Dax:** I reached in the cage and took it out. It seemed happy.

**Wendy:** I think I want to buy a fish.

**Dax:** No more dogs for you?

**Wendy:** I hear fish are less work.

**Dax:** My friend Mark has several. He said his fish haven't caused any problems yet.

**Wendy:** A lot of people love them.

DIALOGUE 14

# Island Life

**Camille:** We have to stay on course. Here you take the wheel.

**Calvin:** What? I can't hear you. There is so much wind.

**Camille:** I said, take the wheel.

**Calvin:** Can you say it again?

**Camille:** TAKE THE WHEEL.

**Calvin:** Ohhh. Okay. I've never been to this island before.

**Camille:** Me neither. Did you see that man on the ship?

**Calvin:** He looks so strong.

**Camille:** Like for real, so in shape. Now, where are we going?

**Calvin:** They said to go north. All these roads will lead us there.

**Camille:** Did you check the map?

**Calvin:** What? Can you say it again?

**Camille:** It's such a pain to talk with the wind. I can't hear your voice.

**Calvin:** I can't hear a word. Let's talk later. We will be there in a half hour.

**Camille:** What?

DIALOGUE 15

# I'm Lost

**Jana:** Can you help me?

**Trent:** I will try. Where are you going?

**Jana:** I began this hike at 10am. I reached the top of the mountain, now I want to go back to my car to go home.

**Trent:** You have covered a lot of ground today.

**Jana:** I have. I am suddenly feeling so tired.

**Trent:** Do you see that cross through the trees?

**Jana:** I do. It's about a hundred yards away.

**Trent:** Exactly. Keep going straight and then take the second path after it, on the right.

**Jana:** Will that lead me to the main trail?

**Trent:** It will. If you ran it would only take about 10 minutes.

**Jana:** I will walk. It's still light out and my feet are sore.

**Trent:** Well you should get back down the mountain in record time.

**Jana:** Thanks so much. I can't wait to take my shoes off.

**Trent:** You're almost to the end. Keep going.

**Jana:** I knew I was close. Thanks for your help.

**Trent:** No problem. Have a good one.

**Jana:** You too!

DIALOGUE 16

# Emergency, Help!

**Doctor:** What seems to be the problem?

**Patient:** I am sick. My head really hurts.

**Doctor:** Your temperature is under 100.

**Patient:** Yesterday it was over 102.

**Doctor:** That could cause some pain.

**Patient:** Something doesn't add up.

**Doctor:** Tell me more. Do you have a list of other symptoms?

**Patient:** Aches, I have a dry cough, but only late at night.

**Doctor:** It could be a number of things. Let me run some tests.

**Patient:** Okay. Can I put my coat on the table here?

**Doctor:** I'm going to have you carry it to the next room. It's just a few steps away.

**Patient:** Yes, that's close enough.

**Doctor:** Don't worry. We will come up with a plan to help you.

**Patient:** Thank you doctor.

**Doctor:** It's what I'm here for.

DIALOGUE 17

# Scheduling a Dentist Appointment

**Receptionist:** Westview Dentistry. How can I help you?

**Mary:** I need to get my teeth cleaned.

**Receptionist:** Have you been here before?

**Mary:** Not yet. It will be my first time.

**Receptionist:** No problem. I will send you some forms online so you won't have to wait in line when you come. What's your email?

**Mary:** Okay, I can fill them out today. It's marynicks@gmail.com

**Receptionist:** Perfect. Are you able to come next Tuesday at 10 or Thursday at 3?

**Mary:** Let me check. It appears that I have Tuesday off work.

**Receptionist:** Perfect. Be sure to complete the forms, every page, and I will see you then.

**Mary:** Thank you.

**Receptionist:** Do you have any other questions?

**Mary:** I don't think so.

**Receptionist:** Okay, well have a great day!

**Mary:** Thanks, you too!

DIALOGUE 18

# Canceling a Hair Appointment

**Receptionist:** Taylor's Barber. How can I help you?

**Todd:** Hi, yes, I have to cancel my son's hair cut today.

**Receptionist:** Ok. What's your boy's name?

**Todd:** Ben Parker.

**Receptionist:** He's supposed to come in an hour. It's a late notice, but it can be done.

**Todd:** Thank you. He has a fever that went above 101.

**Receptionist:** Oh, that's high. Please take care of him.

**Todd:** Thanks. I had him stay home from school. He is resting.

**Receptionist:** Oh good. Do you want to reschedule?

**Todd:** If you don't mind, maybe the same time next week?

**Receptionist:** Yes, we just had a recent cancellation so it's possible. We look forward to serving you.

**Todd:** Thanks. Have a great day.

DIALOGUE 19

# Doctor's Appointment

**Doctor:** Okay, let's take a look at that foot.

**Randy:** I think I have a piece of rock in it.

**Doctor:** Now how did that happen?

**Randy:** I run some big machines at work. We were trying to remove some trees from the ground. When I got off the machine and stepped down, I felt something go through my shoe into my foot.

**Doctor:** Ouch. Have you applied any heat or ice?

**Randy:** No, it's too painful.

**Doctor:** The fact is, there is a small object in your foot. It looks like wood.

**Randy:** Oh no.

**Doctor:** It's a small piece so I think I can remove it real quick.

**Randy:** Ouch!!

**Doctor:** Done. It's the size of a quarter. It happened from the force of your step.

**Randy:** I can't believe it.

**Doctor:** I cleaned the whole thing, but you need to rest for a few days.

**Randy:** I will, thanks Doctor.

DIALOGUE 20

# First Time Waxing

**Esthetician:** What can I do for you today?

**Heather:** I'd like to have my legs waxed.

**Esthetician:** Have you been here before?

**Heather:** No, it's my first time. I'm nervous.

**Esthetician:** That's normal. I'll be direct. It will be painful but not for long.

**Heather:** How does it work?

**Esthetician:** I will use both waxing strips and hot wax that I will press into your legs. Then I will pull it off. I will be done in about one hour.

**Heather:** Will it leave any marks?

**Esthetician:** Typically not.

**Heather:** How much does it cost?

**Esthetician:** $70

**Heather:** A part of me wants to do it, but the other part doesn't.

**Esthetician:** I understand. Well I have time right now. But the rest of the day I am booked.

**Heather:** Okay, let's just go for it.

**Esthetician:** We'll listen to some music. It will put your mind at ease.

**Heather:** Thank you!

DIALOGUE 21

# Spa Day

**Pat:** This has to be the best spa on earth.

**Jill:** I know! All the surfaces are white and gold. It's beautiful.

**Pat:** The last time I was here they gave me the best massage.

**Jill:** That sounds wonderful. What are you going to do this time?

**Pat:** I asked them to fill the bath. It contains volcanic mud.

**Jill:** I want to try a body wrap. It's supposed to help tighten my figure.

**Pat:** I am so happy. I needed this day.

**Jill:** Me too. I mean there has been so much going on with work, I just need to relax.

**Pat:** Yes, as a rule, let's come here once a year.

**Jill:** I agree. It's out of state for me but only an hour away by car.

**Pat:** That's close. Ready to relax?

**Jill:** Absolutely. We're on the same page.

DIALOGUE 22

# Eye Doctors

**Doctor:** Can you read this letter for me?

**Patient:** A or hmm, maybe an E?

**Doctor:** What about this line?

**Patient:** M, E, umm, P, X?

**Doctor:** I will change the order. Look below. What do you see?

**Patient:** D, O, P?

**Doctor:** Now let's look at this pattern. What do you see?

**Patient:** A star, a ball, a plane, a star, a ball, and a plane.

**Doctor:** The ball is actually a moon.

**Patient:** Oh! Among them all, it was the hardest to see.

**Doctor:** I do think you need some glasses. Your left eye is weaker than the right.

**Patient:** I thought maybe I needed glasses.

**Doctor:** Cover your left eye with your hand. Can you read this sentence?

**Patient:** I can't.

**Doctor:** Okay, cover the right eye now. Do you see the object that's in the box?

**Patient:** Hmm, it looks like a tail.

**Doctor:** It's a horse, so it does have a tail. But let me get you some glasses that will help you to see much better.

**Patient:** Thank you doctor.

DIALOGUE 23

# What Movie Should We Watch?

**Calvin:** I think Netflix produced this one.

**Camille:** Oh, I'm reading now that it was filmed in our state!

**Calvin:** It's about a power struggle between a newly married couple.

**Camille:** They are competing for the same job.

**Calvin:** But then one of them broke their leg. It changed everything.

**Camille:** Hmm, could be interesting.

**Calvin:** Or there is this one, it was filmed at a port.

**Camille:** What's it about?

**Calvin:** About some soldiers that have to face each other again after war.

**Camille:** That sounds too sad.

**Calvin:** As usual, you win. Let's watch the first one.

**Camille:** I just think the first one will be better.

**Calvin:** You're probably right.

DIALOGUE 24

# What Would You Like For Dinner?

**Liam:** Well, dinner won't make itself. What would you like?

**Rachel:** We had plain rice last night. What about fish?

**Liam:** Sure. I can teach you how to cook.

**Rachel:** Aren't you a self taught cook?

**Liam:** Yep. I mean I had a bit of a base. My mother was a great cook.

**Rachel:** Do you think men or women are better cooks?

**Liam:** I think any person can be a good cook.

**Rachel:** Without a doubt.

**Liam:** Here, you measure the spices. I will wash and cut some carrots.

**Rachel:** Sure!

**Liam:** After you're done, you can bring me some little, round potatoes. They are behind the basket under the sink.

**Rachel:** Yes. Perhaps we should eat outside. You have a table out there right?

**Liam:** I do. It's warm and it's not dark yet. It will be a special moment.

**Rachel:** My heart is full.

DIALOGUE 25

# Cleaning the Bathroom

**Sara:** I can show you what to do.

**Carlo:** I think this is a two person job.

**Sara:** Haha, yes it might take all day.

**Carlo:** Everything is a mess. We need to clean the whole area.

**Sara:** There was a family that stayed here from out of state.

**Carlo:** How long were they here?

**Sara:** A few months. Look at this toilet water. It's green.

**Carlo:** I'm happy to help. Give me something to do.

**Sara:** Okay, let's bring some order to this room. Can you wipe the surfaces down?

**Carlo:** The sink?

**Sara:** Yes and also the front of the cabinet and under it too.

**Carlo:** Of course. This is hard work, I'm glad you don't have to do it alone.

**Sara:** We're in this together. It may take all night but after we can go eat.

**Carlo:** Sure, I know a great place right up the road, just a few minutes from here.

**Sara:** Tacos? I remember that place! We ate there a long time ago.

**Carlo:** That's the one!

DIALOGUE 26

# Doing the Laundry

**Matt:** Mom, I'm home, with my laundry.

**Mom:** Hi son! Do you ever wash your clothes at college?

**Matt:** I'm a broke college student.

**Mom:** Haha, I'm almost finished with dinner, then I can help you.

**Matt:** I can divide them into whites and darks.

**Mom:** Oh! I found a red shirt between these white ones.

**Matt:** Oh! You found it? I bought it last week but then I lost it. I knew it had to be somewhere.

**Mom:** It's nice. Are you going to sleep here? Do you have to study?

**Matt:** I will study. I already began to study science but I must also start with history.

**Mom:** I will give you some time. I will wash and dry your clothes and let you know when they are ready.

**Matt:** You're the best.

DIALOGUE 27

# Emptying the Dishwasher

**Marge:** I can do this myself if you want to water the plants.

**Pat:** I already did. You made lunch, let me serve too.

**Marge:** Okay, you can carry those plates and place them above the cups.

**Pat:** Good idea. You can't reach that high.

**Marge:** Haha, true. I will do everything down low.

**Pat:** Look at the trees in the wind.

**Marge:** Summer storms. I think it came from the north.

**Pat:** Probably. They are strong, but over quick.

**Marge:** I wouldn't mind going for the mile walk to the river after.

**Pat:** Good idea. The air is always fresh after a storm.

**Marge:** The view of the sun over the mountains is my favorite.

**Pat:** I like to move after we eat.

**Marge:** It's nice to listen to the sound of the birds.

**Pat:** It's better than music.

**Marge:** It's good for the heart, body, and mind.

DIALOGUE 28

# Making Breakfast

**Calvin:** We have to feed six kids on a short notice.

**Camille:** But I am happy we can help.

**Calvin:** Same. How should we do it? Thoughts?

**Camille:** Maybe we can have them form a line.

**Calvin:** I already took note of what we need to buy.

**Camille:** Great. Maybe I can start cooking.

**Calvin:** What did you decide on?

**Camille:** Pancakes with fruit.

**Calvin:** Nice. We need to appear calm so they don't cry.

**Camille:** They miss their mom. She is having another baby now.

**Calvin:** There are 3 boys and 3 girls. At least they have each other.

**Camille:** I hope there will be enough food.

**Calvin:** Don't worry. We can take care of them.

**Camille:** They are almost here.

**Calvin:** I will open the door.

DIALOGUE 29

# Curfew

**Mom:** Remember, no later than 11pm.

**Bryce:** Is it possible to stay out later? Ivy is finally free. She has been so busy.

**Mom:** Are you going to drive or take the train?

**Bryce:** I will drive to her house and then we will go by bus actually.

**Mom:** Okay. I guess you can stay out until 12, since it's the weekend.

**Bryce:** Thanks. We're going to the city center. Ivy has an interest in learning a new language and there is a special meetup group.

**Mom:** Does she go often?

**Bryce:** It's a little far from her home, so it's not so usual for her to go.

**Mom:** Well I will turn the porch light on for you. I won't wait up though.

**Bryce:** It's okay. You can go to bed, sleep is important. I'll see you in the morning.

**Mom:** Have fun. Tell Ivy hi. Love you.

**Bryce:** Love you mom!

DIALOGUE 30

# On the Moon

**Son:** We're going to the surface of the moon dad.

**Dad:** How will we get there, a plane?

**Son:** No, a big black rocket.

**Dad:** The moon is pretty far away.

**Son:** Are there rocks on the moon dad? Will we see the sun from there?

**Dad:** I'm sure we'll see rocks, maybe not much life though.

**Son:** Do people live on the moon?

**Dad:** No son, but we can just pretend and play.

**Son:** Can we eat? I will go get us some moon food.

**Dad:** Sure, anything is possible.

DIALOGUE 31

# Homework

**Mom:** I thought you liked your class this year.

**Maddox:** I do, but I have a list of things to complete.

**Mom:** Like what?

**Maddox:** I have to read part of my science book. I have to answer the questions. I have to write several sentences.

**Mom:** That is a number of things. Why don't you ask your father to help?

**Maddox:** Where is dad?

**Mom:** He ran across the street to play some ball. He should be back soon.

**Maddox:** I'm going to sit down and get started. I just remembered I have to add some numbers for math class and learn how to spell some words for English class.

**Mom:** Your teacher gave you a lot of work.

**Maddox:** I told you.

**Mom:** You're going to become even smarter. Remember that story you wrote last month about that blue plane found on that wild island?

**Maddox:** Yeah...what about it?

**Mom:** There was such beauty and creativity in it. I love your spirit.

**Maddox:** You are kind, mom. I'm happy you're my mother.

DIALOGUE 32

# I'm Sick

**Nurse:** Did someone call me?

**Shelly:** Yes. Do you know when this ship will be to the next port?

**Nurse:** It will still be a while. We have to cross over these final hundred miles west. We are traveling the world.

**Shelly:** I just want to be on solid ground again. How long before the next town?

**Nurse:** Probably 5 hours. You should try to lie on the bed with your feet up.

**Shelly:** I would do anything to feel better.

**Nurse:** When did you begin to feel sick?

**Shelly:** I don't remember. I took a pill though.

**Nurse:** Oh, please don't cry. If you can hold on a little longer, it should pass.

**Shelly:** Nothing seems to ease this feeling.

**Nurse:** Take slow breaths. Rest your eyes. Eat plain foods. If anything happens, please call me again.

**Shelly:** Thanks. I'm just mad. It's such a pain being sick. I want to enjoy the heat and the sun.

**Nurse:** Don't worry. I'm certain you will get better fast.

DIALOGUE 33

# I'm Late for School

**Mom:** Well now you can't go to school by bike.

**John:** I was working on that paper last night.

**Mom:** It's the second time you're late this week.

**John:** I know. What's the cat doing outside?

**Mom:** Open the door and let it in.

**John:** Can you drive me to school?

**Mom:** Yes, but you have to come up with a plan so that you're not late.

**John:** I wish I could fly, but it's not so simple.

**Mom:** Haha. Do you have a test today?

**John:** No, but can I have some money for lunch?

**Mom:** Fine, but for the record, it's going to be the last time this week.

**John:** Thanks. I will stop asking. I don't want to cause a fight.

**Mom:** You may need a new job, even something near the house, to help you earn some money.

**John:** Yes. Thanks for being direct. I will follow your advice.

**Mom:** Now let's go.

DIALOGUE 34

# Walk the Dog

**Britney:** What's your favorite animal?

**Mitch:** My dog of course. You?

**Britney:** If I lived in the country like you, I would say the same because this field is amazing.

**Mitch:** Yes, my dog loves to run here. Plus I get my daily steps in.

**Britney:** What's your dog's name again?

**Mitch:** Black, because he is black. Haha

**Britney:** You have a great laugh. I thought I heard someone sing a song, listen.

**Mitch:** I think it's just the birds. During the summer, they sing a lot.

**Britney:** You have so much land, what grows here?

**Mitch:** Well, I wanted to plant a garden but now I'm building a small house.

**Britney:** What's that? It looks like a wheel to an old boat.

**Mitch:** Hmm, no, look at that star pattern. It's from a machine of some kind.

**Britney:** Should we head back?

**Mitch:** Sure. We've been out here long enough. Also, I am hungry.

**Britney:** Let's go this way, along this road, towards the woods.

**Mitch:** Okay, after you. Come on Black, let's go.

DIALOGUE 35

# Christmas

**Jess:** Among all the American holidays, Christmas is my favorite.

**Jer:** I saw some very green trees that were priced half off.

**Jess:** I will clear my schedule, let's go!

**Jer:** I think it will snow tomorrow.

**Jess:** They say 10 inches to a foot.

**Jer:** A few miles east of here already got 6 inches.

**Jess:** We will have to put a fire going.

**Jer:** I love a good fire. Which road am I on?

**Jess:** Turn left on that road up ahead.

**Jer:** Oh yeah, I remember seeing this on the map.

**Jess:** Follow it to the end and we're there.

**Jer:** It came up so suddenly.

**Jess:** Pull in here. Now it's time for some Christmas spirit.

**Jer:** I am full of wonder this year.

## DIALOGUE 36

# Babysitting

**Babysitter:** Do you want to draw a picture or play a game?

**Little boy:** I like to draw the moon and earth.

**Babysitter:** Okay, or you can draw your hand. How many fingers do you have?

**Little boy:** I already know. One, two, three, four, five.

**Babysitter:** Good. I will point to a letter and you tell me what it is.

**Little boy:** Six.

**Babysitter:** That's a number. We're doing letters. It's a b.

**Little boy:** Oh yeah. Well I know a thousand shapes.

**Babysitter:** I'm sure you do. What's this one down below?

**Little boy:** It looks like a rock.

**Babysitter:** It does! What color is it?

**Little boy:** Gold or yellow.

**Babysitter:** You're so smart. How about you draw your foot now?

**Little boy:** I am drawing a real monkey with a tail.

**Babysitter:** Haha, okay whatever you want.

DIALOGUE 37

# The Lost Bunny

**Little girl:** I have his carrot, but I can't find him.

**Mother:** Stand up, maybe he's under you.

**Little girl:** I already stood up. He's not under me.

**Mother:** Did he fall behind something?

**Little girl:** No. He's probably sad.

**Mother:** Let's mark where you looked.

**Little girl:** I looked everywhere.

**Mother:** What about under the bed in your room?

**Little girl:** Not there.

**Mother:** He is so tiny in size. He doesn't even weigh more than two pounds.

**Little girl:** Oh, I finally found him.

**Mother:** Oh my. It got itself stuck under my cleaning products. How did this happen?

**Little girl:** No idea. I came to your rescue bunny!

**Mother:** You sure did.

DIALOGUE 38

# Baking a Cake

**Myles:** Does this cake contain eggs?

**Camille:** Yes, and it has less milk than normal cakes.

**Myles:** I tried the best cake last week.

**Camille:** Really? What kind?

**Myles:** It's name was "deep dark chocolate dream".

**Camille:** Wow, that's quite the name.

**Myles:** It was my favorite.

**Camille:** It sounds great. Here, you measure the flour.

**Myles:** Okay. And butter?

**Camille:** Oh, yes, I almost forgot.

**Myles:** I will mix it all.

**Camille:** The oven is ready. You can put it in.

**Myles:** I can't wait to try it.

DIALOGUE 39

# Spilled Milk

**Danny:** Mom, I spilled the milk.

**Mom:** Again?

**Danny:** I can clean it on my own.

**Mom:** Careful you don't slip and fall.

**Danny:** Can you hand me some paper towel?

**Mom:** Here, press this on the floor to soak it up.

**Danny:** It's clean.

**Mom:** Let me wipe it with some soap and water.

**Danny:** Can I have more milk?

**Mom:** Sure.

DIALOGUE 40

# Out on the Boat

**Peter:** I'm so glad you came. I didn't want to force you.

**Trish:** Me too. You didn't. I want to develop and grow as a person.

**Peter:** I know you are scared of being on the water,  but you will be fine.

**Trish:** I know it's not a common problem, but I am a little afraid.

**Peter:** The main thing is, not to think about it so much.

**Trish:** True. Look at the sunny, blue sky.

**Peter:** The birds are singing their songs.

**Trish:** Suddenly I feel so happy. I'm at ease.

**Peter:** That's great. We'll take the boat a few miles south.

**Trish**: To the port?

**Peter:** Exactly. Then we'll get some lunch in the center of the city.

**Trish:** I'll check google maps for a good place to eat.

**Peter:** Good idea. Then let's enjoy this special moment.

DIALOGUE 41

# Road Trip

**Jasper:** What objects are in that box of yours anyways?

**June:** A lot of gold.

**Jasper:** Haha, I wondered because of the weight.

**June:** No, I just have a lot of books.

**Jasper:** I thought you were done with college.

**June:** Almost. I have to study both science and history over the summer.

**Jasper:** I thought you wanted to learn a new language?

**June:** Yeah, but we're going to spend a lot of time in the car. We can listen and learn.

**Jasper:** True, I want to learn with you. I'll follow your lead.

**June:** I will act like I know what I am doing.

**Jasper:** Haha, you rule, it's a fact!

**June:** You're funny. Shall we go?

**Jasper:** If possible, I need to go to the bathroom real quick.

**June:** Yes, go! We won't stop for at least 3 hours.

**Jasper:** Okay, I'll be right back.

DIALOGUE 42

# Weekend Getaway

**Ivory:** Should we go out to the country or near the sea?

**Sam:** The sea is four hours away by car.

**Ivory:** But it's winter, it might rain or there might be wind.

**Sam:** I already checked. It's going to be sunny.

**Ivory:** We can ride bikes and rest.

**Sam:** Oh, we could ride horses.

**Ivory:** Yes. Horses help me get in touch with my inner self.

**Sam**: Wow really?

**Ivory:** Yes, I feel so wild and free when I ride them.

**Sam:** I can see that. They are so powerful.

**Ivory:** We should get a room with a view of the sea.

**Sam:** My thoughts exactly.

**Ivory:** I can't wait to spend time together, just us.

**Sam:** I agree.

DIALOGUE 43

# Catching Up

**Sierra:** It's been so long, how are you?

**Austin:** I'm doing great, how about you?

**Sierra:** So well. I am a teacher now.

**Austin:** No way, what school?

**Sierra:** Can you believe I'm at the one we went to, right down the street from my house?

**Austin:** That's amazing, you can easily bike or walk there. It's only a minute away.

**Sierra:** I know. The students are great. My mother and father moved away, so I bought their old house.

**Austin:** Wow. That worked out.

**Sierra:** Yes. What are you up to?

**Austin:** I work at a huge American company. We produce parts for planes and trains.

**Sierra:** Wow, so there must be a lot of big machines there.

**Austin:** Exactly. We produce a thousand pieces every week.

**Sierra:** Well I would love to talk more over dinner.

**Austin:** Me too, perhaps tomorrow night?

**Sierra:** Sounds good.

DIALOGUE 44

# Airport Check-in

**Front desk clerk:** Hi. Can I see your I.D. please?

**Tom:** Sure, here you go.

**Front desk clerk:** Thanks. I see you're going to New York. How many bags are you checking?

**Tom:** None. I just have my carry-on.

**Front desk clerk:** Okay. Here is your boarding pass. Your plane is leaving in one hour.

**Tom:** Great, hopefully security is quick.

**Front desk clerk:** It should be. A big group passed through but that was twenty minutes ago.

**Tom:** Okay. At least I don't have to run.

**Front desk clerk:** Not at all. Cross that hall and you will reach the security checkpoint.

DIALOGUE 45

# Asking for Directions

**August:** Excuse me, where is the train station?

**Random Stranger:** Cross the street over there, take a right heading south, walk along that road for about six minutes and it will be on your left.

**August:** Thanks so much. Listen, can I ask you another question?

**Random Stranger:** Sure. I don't mind.

**August:** I'm going to LA city center. Do I need to change lines or does the train go directly there?

**Random Stranger:** It's direct and it passes about every half hour.

**August:** Great. I've never been here before, but the people seem great.

**Random Stranger:** Most of them are. Enjoy your time.

**August:** Oh, one more thing, how much money do I need for a ticket?

**Random Stranger:** Well, it's not free, but I can't remember because I usually drive. It should be less than $5.

**August:** Okay, no problem. Thanks again.

DIALOGUE 46

# Shopping

**Lily:** Why are you writing a letter?

**Mom:** I'm actually making a list.

**Lily:** For the store?

**Mom:** Yes, can you think of anything you want?

**Lily:** Green and red apples.

**Mom:** Okay. Oh yeah, that reminds me, I also need some cleaning products.

**Lily:** Can I come with you?

**Mom:** I suppose. Your father is staying home with your baby brother while he sleeps.

**Lily:** I'll go put on my shoes.

**Mom:** Okay, I want to leave as soon as possible.

**Lily:** Mom, I opened the door. I'm waiting.

**Mom:** Coming. Oh wow, it's warm out today. The sun feels nice.

DIALOGUE 47

# Saying No

**David:** You have my answer. I don't think it will work this time.

**Bree:** But for once I thought you would say yes.

**David:** Maybe if it was not on a school night.

**Bree:** I feel so mad and like you don't care.

**David:** Of course I care. I just think this is for the best.

**Bree:** The whole group will be there, all my friends.

**David:** I heard. It wasn't easy for me to decide.

**Bree:** They will probably play games.

**David:** It's the end of the day, I don't want to fight.

**Bree:** Can't you change your mind dad?

**David:** No. Please don't cry. Remember, I always have your best interest in mind.

DIALOGUE 48

# Let's play Tennis

**Julia:** I told you, I'm not very good.

**Sam:** I won't laugh.

**Julia:** See, I always hit the ball too low.

**Sam:** Try to put a little more power in your swing.

**Julia:** Better?

**Sam:** You have good form. I have a plan to get you in even better shape.

**Julia:** Come on, I'm already strong.

**Sam:** True. You're young and you have a great figure.

**Julia:** So what's your plan?

**Sam:** We start to run every other morning before school.

**Julia:** We can develop a real plan if you're open to it.

**Sam:** Of course. Let's begin now. We can practice hitting the ball.

**Julia:** For the record, I can start to keep notes of my progress.

**Sam:** Great idea. We can start to lift weights too. Do you know your weight?

**Julia:** I don't. Maybe 130 pounds.

**Sam:** No worries. We can check later.

DIALOGUE 49

# Language Learning

**London:** You speak several languages right?

**Jude:** I do. I'm taking a Japanese class now. I learned some languages by myself.

**London:** Do you read books or listen to music?

**Jude:** Both. First, I try to learn the letters, listen to the sounds, and form common sentences.

**London:** That's awesome. I'm having a hard time learning Spanish. Part of me wants to quit. I don't know if I can be self-taught.

**Jude:** You could try to live with a Spanish speaking family. Children can teach you so much.

**London:** Have you done it?

**Jude:** I'm living with a Japanese family now. They always correct me because they know I want to learn well. I like when people point out my mistakes though.

**London:** Maybe I will do that. For now I'm reading a short story every night.

**Jude:** The main thing is being consistent and you should laugh a lot.

**London:** I think I have to. It's that or cry.

DIALOGUE 50

# Memories

**Jocelyn:** Remember when you broke mom's blue vase she got during her travels?

**Dale:** And I thought she wouldn't notice.

**Jocelyn:** You just stood there.

**Dale:** The table was a huge mess, pieces everywhere.

**Jocelyn:** And then we heard mom's voice.

**Dale:** I knew she would be mad, so I ran.

**Jocelyn:** Me too. I could hear her coming. I was in complete shock.

**Dale:** I could not move or say anything. I tried to cover my head.

**Jocelyn:** We were pressed in the back of the closet behind our clothes.

**Dale:** I was against the wall, just waiting for mom to appear.

**Jocelyn:** She was so kind though. She didn't even make you buy her a new vase.

**Dale:** I felt terrible. Did you know I brought her one back from Italy last year?

**Jocelyn:** I didn't. How funny. Good memories.

DIALOGUE 51

# Fishing

**Kate:** Well you're the best person to teach me how to fish.

**Dad:** This river is perfect. I think Georgia has the best rivers for fishing.

**Kate:** What was the largest fish you ever caught?

**Dad:** Around a foot long.

**Kate:** Wow. Oh look, a dog, my favorite animal.

**Dad:** With no owner. Hmm.

**Kate:** Oh, I see a man over there behind those trees.

**Dad:** He's coming towards us now, probably looking for his dog.

**Kate:** The dog is so happy wagging his tail.

**Dad:** He is. The ground is still soft from that rain last night.

**Kate:** Is that good?

**Dad:** It means the fish should be hungry.

DIALOGUE 52

# Eating Out

**Waitress:** Would you like your burger with or without cheese?

**Daniel:** With. Hold that thought. Does it contain lactose?

**Waitress**: It does.

**Daniel:** Okay then, without!

**Waitress:** Okay. Now the fun part, you can come to the back. I will show you the box where we plant vegetables and I will cut some herbs for your salad.

**Daniel:** Wow. You grow your own food?

**Waitress:** Almost everything. Everything is made here at the restaurant. Our local farmers bring us fresh food too.

**Daniel:** That's so cool.

**Waitress:** It's part of the reason I love my job so much.

**Daniel:** What else do you love about your job?

**Waitress:** The second thing is that I see the same people. They come often.

**Daniel:** That's special. That must mean you are close to them.

**Waitress:** I really am. Well, let me go put your order in.

DIALOGUE 53

# Appetizers

**Gabe:** I'm so glad you were able to meet me.

**Lila:** Island life, I wouldn't miss it. But this town was hard to find.

**Gabe:** It's barely on the map. But the food is great.

**Lila:** I saw a waterfall about a hundred yards east of here, wait, no west.

**Gabe:** We can walk there after if you want.

**Lila:** Sure, but first, since we're here, what should we order?

**Gabe:** I'm a little full, but I won't say no to their wild salmon.

**Lila:** The mushrooms sound good to me.

**Gabe:** Hmm which one is better?

**Lila:** Let's get both.

**Gabe:** Yes! Let's enjoy the night. Nothing can stop us.

**Lila:** I'm glad we found each other.

DIALOGUE 54

# Lunch with a Colleague

**Jan:** I'm certain I've been here before. I remember the high ceilings and the round tables.

**Martha:** I love the colors and patterns on the tables.

**Jan:** Plus it feels cozy with the fire down below.

**Martha:** A girl on the bus told me about this place.

**Jan:** I am glad I could clear my schedule. I've been so busy.

**Martha:** Really? Work has been slow for me.

**Jan:** It's still early in the month, it may still get busy.

**Martha:** True. I began to send weekly emails. I'm hoping to fill some spots.

**Jan:** You have until when?

**Martha:** Who knows. Maybe until May.

**Jan:** Well among all the people I know, you're one of the best workers I know.

**Martha:** Thank you for your kind words.

**Jan:** Are you ready to order?

**Martha:** Let's do it.

DIALOGUE 55

# Ordering a Pizza

**Marika:** My friend gave me the name of this place. She lives above their restaurant and said they serve the best pizza.

**Lucas:** Wow. We should order. I'm hungry. When I'm hungry I become angry.

**Marika:** I'm going to call. What kind of pizza should I order?

**Lucas:** My usual, deep crust pepperoni and black olives on top.

**Marika**: What size?

**Lucas:** Large.

**Marika:** Okay. I prefer plain cheese.

**Lucas:** Should we get anything on the side?

**Marika:** No, but while we wait we can go for a walk in the field behind our house.

**Lucas:** The surface of the ground looks wet. I prefer to keep my feet dry.

**Marika:** What about rain boots?

**Lucas:** We can go down the street and walk past the port. It's still light out.

**Marika:** Yeah, let's go before the sun sets.

DIALOGUE 56

# The Drive-thru

**Josh:** We're next in line.

**Jill:** Did you see that car ahead of us has five men? Or boys, I can't tell.

**Josh:** I think they are students. There is a university right down the road.

**Jill:** Correct! You're right. I forgot about that. Can you order me a green salad?

**Josh:** Sure. I am going to pull up to the window now.

**Employee:** Welcome. What can I get for you?

**Josh:** Hi. A green salad and a hamburger, plain. Plus two waters.

**Employee:** And as your side?

**Josh:** I guess fries.

**Employee:** Anything else?

**Josh:** No, that's all.

**Employee:** That will be $10.49. Please pull up to the next window.

**Josh:** Great thanks.

DIALOGUE 57

# Grocery Store

**Ryder:** I'm telling you, it's the best store on earth.

**Jess:** Why do you say that?

**Ryder:** It sells products from all over the world.

**Jess:** Okay, I'm ready to check it out.

**Ryder:** Turn left, don't turn your head, keep your eyes straight ahead.

**Jess:** Wait, what is that?

**Ryder:** It's an area where they let you try all kinds of food.

**Jess:** I'm so happy now. Wow, there is so much beauty in this food.

**Ryder:** Come on, it's not gonna try itself. Let's eat.

**Jess:** What's your age again?

**Ryder:** 22, why?

**Jess:** Because they have wine samples too!

**Ryder:** I told you it's the best. This day will mark your life. Trust me.

**Jess:** It already has!

DIALOGUE 58

# At the Supermarket

**Miranda:** I can't reach the box, can you get it for me?

**Gabriel:** I don't see it.

**Miranda:** It's up high, above the red box.

**Gabriel:** Oh, yes. There you go.

**Miranda:** What else do we need?

**Gabriel:** We're low on milk and I thought we could buy some plants.

**Miranda:** To put where?

**Gabriel:** Maybe the living room. I love to see more green.

**Miranda:** True, it gives the room a more zen feeling.

**Gabriel:** I think that's the last thing on the list.

**Miranda:** Should we go check out?

## DIALOGUE 59

# Tardy

**Teacher:** You're late. Wait, are you even in my class?

**Student:** Yes, sorry. I'm a new foreign exchange student.

**Teacher:** Oh. Welcome to history class. What's your name?

**Student:** Sung-Kim.

**Teacher:** Can you spell that?

**Student:** Sure. S-u-n-g-k-i-m.

**Teacher:** What country are you from?

**Student:** Korea.

**Teacher:** Great. Maybe you could point to it on the map?

**Student:** Sure. It's there. I might add that it's very far from America.

**Teacher:** Indeed. What's a fun fact about Korea?

**Student:** We are considered one year old when we are born.

**Teacher:** Wow. Well I'm sure we'll learn many things from you.

**Student:** And I will from you.

**Teacher:** Class, let's turn to page ten in your history books and we can start by reading the examples.

DIALOGUE 60

# At Dance School

**Sally:** It's a simple move really.

**Maddox:** I can't follow your lead.

**Sally:** It's your left foot that's causing the problem.

**Maddox:** And my right foot?

**Sally:** It's doing the right thing, no pun intended.

**Maddox:** Haha. Let's go again. I will try my best.

**Sally:** Okay, left foot first, to the front. Right foot next to the front.

**Maddox:** And to the back, now spin around.

**Sally:** Turn to the left, good, now to the right, great.

**Maddox:** So simple. Haha, not at all. But I'm starting to follow.

**Sally:** Then we move up, now we go down. Turn around. And from the top.

**Maddox:** I will act like I know what I'm doing.

**Sally:** That's the spirit.

DIALOGUE 61

# School Cafeteria

**John:** Come sit over here with us.

**Tiffany:** Oh hi! I didn't see you.

**John:** How's your day been?

**Tiffany:** I've had a hard day, well week really.

**John:** Oh, why?

**Tiffany:** I have so many papers to write. Not to mention I have to draw 3 pictures for my art class. I'm so busy.

**John:** I'm sure you will get it all done. You have until when?

**Tiffany:** I have time. Maybe we could help each other?

**John:** We can study together. You can ask me questions from my science book. Then I have to build a model earth.

**Tiffany:** Good idea. Maybe you can think of some sentences for my papers.

**John:** For sure. But first things first, let's eat lunch.

DIALOGUE 62

# Enrolling a New Student

**School Secretary:** What's your son's name?

**Parent:** Doug.

**School Secretary:** What's his age?

**Parent:** He is ten.

**School Secretary:** Okay. And you said he has a brother?

**Parent:** Yes, but he is still a baby.

**School Secretary:** Oh okay, so Doug is the only one in school?

**Parent:** That's correct.

**School Secretary:** Do you have a record of his report card from his last school?

**Parent:** I do. Right here.

**School Secretary:** Great. Can you fill out this form?

**Parent:** Sure.

**School Secretary:** Great. I am going to mark a few things as a note to myself.

**Parent:** Sure. You are certain Doug can start school tomorrow?

**School Secretary:** No problem. He can come.

**Parent:** He will be so happy.

DIALOGUE 63

# Principal's Office

**Father:** So what is this about?

**Principal:** Like I said in my call, your son has been the cause of many problems in class.

**Father:** He has many friends and he makes them laugh.

**Principal:** But he doesn't follow the rules. He acts out of line.

**Father:** I'm sorry to hear this.

**Principal:** For example, he arrives late to class and is slow to listen. He disrupts the other students. Something needs to change.

**Father:** What's the answer?

**Principal:** If you agree, we can work together to develop a morning routine and he can be part of an after school group.

**Father:** I don't want to force him, but I do want to help him.

**Principal:** If you decide to do this, I am sure we will notice big changes.

**Father:** Let's try it, at least for a few weeks.

**Principal:** Great. We can even start tomorrow.

DIALOGUE 64

# Parent-teacher Conference

**Teacher:** I am happy that you show interest in your child. I have a number of things to share with you.

**Mother:** Oh great. She is a wonderful girl.

**Teacher:** Samantha has great marks in both science and history. She can read very well.

**Mother:** Those are her favorite classes.

**Teacher:** I want to send home some word lists so that she can work on both writing and spelling. She can take notes and practice writing sentences. I think this will help her. You can correct any mistakes.

**Mother:** How often should we do this and until when?

**Teacher:** If possible, I would like you to practice just ten minutes a day for the next four to five weeks.

**Mother:** I can make that happen.

**Teacher:** She is young and will learn fast. I am certain.

DIALOGUE 65

# My Favorite Class

**Janelle:** American history has been fun even though it's been a lot of work.

**Lawrence:** Art has become my favorite class.

**Janelle:** Since I'm not so creative, I lean towards history and science.

**Lawrence:** Perhaps you need to give it a try. There are hundreds of things you can do.

**Janelle:** I used to draw pictures when I was little.

**Lawrence:** I remember watching my father paint alone in his office for hours.

**Janelle:** What special memories. They must make your heart happy.

**Lawrence:** They do! Sometimes it seems that art comes to life and tells a story.

**Janelle:** It probably would clear my mind too.

**Lawrence:** I just bought some new paints. Come be a part of my world and paint with me tomorrow after school.

**Janelle:** Oh, why not!?

DIALOGUE 66

# What are you Studying?

**Lance:** What are you working on?

**Jules:** I need to write a few more pages for a report and then I will finally be done.

**Lance:** How long have you been working?

**Jules:** Hmm, I've been here on my own for around an hour. I don't always like to work by myself though.

**Lance:** I thought I saw you here during breakfast too, against that wall.

**Jules:** Yes. I began to study early. Then I went home for lunch and came back again.

**Lance:** I don't live far. Do you see where I am pointing? I live behind those green trees along the river.

**Jules:** Oh that's nice. I have to walk through town, going south and pass under the bridge to get home.

**Lance:** Do you ever take the bus?

**Jules:** Only when it snows or rains. I prefer walking.

**Lance:** Do you want to come to my house and play a game after you're done studying?

**Jules:** Yes. Lead the way!

DIALOGUE 67

# Work Meeting

**Boss:** I have done nothing to prepare for this meeting.

**Employee:** It's your second one today right?

**Boss:** Yes, I'm getting tired of these meetings. But I am also trying to build a business.

**Employee:** If you want to rest, I can run the next one.

**Boss:** That would be great. I set all the notes on the round table and you'll find the coffee, ready to make, I measured the water, just press start. You can serve that too.

**Employee:** Which room?

**Boss:** You can use the one below me. I will probably hear you.

**Employee:** I will begin now. If you want to pass by, you can sit or even stand in the back for a few minutes.

**Boss:** I will be near. I have a large amount of forms to complete and letters to write.

**Employee:** I knew you wouldn't rest! You never do.

**Boss:** A business doesn't produce itself.

**Employee:** Fair enough, just get some sleep tonight okay?

DIALOGUE 68

# Staying Late

**Fiona:** You still haven't left yet?

**Trever:** I was ready and suddenly I saw a light appear and I heard a cry.

**Fiona:** Why are you holding a cat?

**Trever:** Actually there were several cats, but this one was all alone. Look at its tail.

**Fiona:** It seems hurt. You're so nice to cover it with your jacket.

**Trever:** I'm going to take it to that vet above our favorite coffee shop.

**Fiona:** Oh yeah. I remember him. The owner is such a nice man and I'm sure he will be able to care for the cat.

**Trever:** It's less than a half mile walk too.

**Fiona:** Well, I'm ready. I'll go with you to ease your mind. Let's see if we can collect any other animals along the way.

**Trever:** Note to self, hang out with Fiona more often.

DIALOGUE 69

# The New Employee

**New Employee:** So this is the ground floor?

**Boss:** Yes. You can see the ships dock there on the port, we fill them with products and then they go to many countries and even islands all around the world.

**New Employee:** Where do the ships come from?

**Boss:** The north, the south, the east, and west.

**New Employee:** So everywhere!

**Boss:** Exactly. We have products from 30 states and most of them are made by hand.

**New Employee:** So my main job is to direct this area here, correct?

**Boss:** Yes. Learn who is who. Every face has a name. I just hired 5 new men. We will have a special day where they can bring their children and we can all go on one of the ships.

**New Employee:** That's so cool. I've only been on a ship once a long time ago.

**Boss:** Soon, I will have you travel once a month, but not yet since it's still winter.

**New Employee:** Well, I think I am all set. Thank you for this opportunity.

DIALOGUE 70

# Breaktime

**Monica:** Among all the places I have worked, this office is my favorite.

**Ross:** I know. It's not common to have a boss like ours. Yesterday I told our boss that I could use a break and he gave me two hours.

**Monica:** I took a week off last month. I'm even more productive than ever.

**Ross:** I'm trying to design these final dress patterns.

**Monica:** Whoa, it's a beauty! I love that deep red color. You should add some gold.

**Ross:** Thanks. Is the shape right? Is it too low cut? I want it to work for all body sizes.

**Monica:** For a woman with a full figure, it might be too low.

**Ross:** Okay, I want it to serve them also.

**Monica:** For the record, it's really great. Look at those sides, and the back too, I give it ten stars.

**Ross:** Thanks girl. I will check with our boss. I wonder what he will think.

DIALOGUE 71

# Phone call to Boss

**Boss:** Can we make this quick Jenny, as usual, I'm up in the air.

**Jenny:** Your voice is so clear.

**Boss:** When I fly, I connect to the internet, so that's how I can carry out calls.

**Jenny:** Okay. Something broke in the copy room. I was only able to print three thousand copies but we need ten thousand.

**Boss:** Sometimes when the machine gets hot, it stops working. I can give you a hand when I land.

**Jenny:** Oh, the heat! That didn't even cross my mind.

**Boss:** Can you work on the file that contains the case for tomorrow?

**Jenny:** Of course.

**Boss:** There is also a box that should have arrived on my desk. Please don't open it.

**Jenny:** What did you buy?

**Boss:** I'll show you later. I'll see you soon.

**Jenny:** Okay!

DIALOGUE 72

# I Quit

**Mark:** The fact is, I had many amazing moments here.

**Boss:** You have stood by me. I've watched you fight hard here. Thank you.

**Mark:** I think my time has come to an end here. I want to be free to try a new field.

**Boss:** As much as I hate to see you go, I don't think you can move up anymore in this company. You've gone as high as you can go.

**Mark:** I know. You helped me get on my feet and I learned so much with you.

**Boss:** You are a strong leader and though I've given you a lot of power, you never took advantage.

**Mark:** Thank you. I feel like I have passed all the tests and it's time that I step into new things.

**Boss:** Yes, you know I'm always here for you if you ever fall.

**Mark:** I will remember!

DIALOGUE 73

# Applying for a Job

**Madison:** As a whole, the company seems amazing.

**Tom:** Tell me about it again.

**Madison:** They create unique objects out of rocks, wood, and metal.

**Tom:** Well, creating is your passion. Why don't you apply?

**Madison:** I got a crazy offer from a boy I went to high school with. We ran against each other for school president.

**Tom:** Oh really?

**Madison:** He has a boat and he wants to take a year to sail around the world.

**Tom:** That is crazy!

**Madison:** You know how much I love the sun and water. Plus, imagine bonfires on the beach.

**Tom:** You never wanted a plain and ordinary life.

**Madison:** I know. I'm over the moon! What should I say?

**Tom:** The ball really is in your court with this one.

DIALOGUE 74

# Follow-up Interview

**Beatrice:** Thank you for having me back.

**Boss:** Yes. We called you back for a second interview because we really loved your voice. You sing beautiful songs.

**Beatrice:** Thank you. Singing is my passion.

**Boss:** We can see that. We would like to hear you sing again, plus we wanted to know if you have any questions about the job, because we only touched the surface.

**Beatrice:** I've had a bit of a dry cough, I hope it doesn't affect my voice.

**Boss:** Don't worry. If you want, you can come back to sing.

**Beatrice:** I was wondering if you could tell me about more of the benefits for this job.

**Boss:** Half of our singers go on to sing professionally after working with us for a year. This job opens many doors to new opportunities.

**Beatrice:** Is there a chance to earn more money? I saw the base pay is a bit low.

**Boss:** After three months, you can get a pay raise, and then again after 6 months.

**Beatrice:** Okay. I think I would like to take it.

**Boss:** That's great news. I'm so happy.

DIALOGUE 75

# I got the Job

**Heather:** I got the job. Can you believe it?

**Carl:** Of course! I knew you would land it.

**Heather:** I know I work hard, but I am still surprised.

**Carl:** You are so small, 110 pounds, so of course, from the surface, people might have not chosen you.

**Heather:** But I play well. I'm strong and I run so fast.

**Carl:** When do you start?

**Heather:** Next week. I have to move across the world.

**Carl:** But Germany is so close to so many countries. You can travel a lot.

**Heather:** I am excited to get to know the other girls on my team.

**Carl:** It's like a new life for you. You will grow so much as a person.

**Heather:** Promise you will call me every day.

**Carl:** Promise.

DIALOGUE 76

# New Responsibilities

**Riana:** I think I am ready too. I have led this group for over a year.

**Boss:** I want to put you in front of everybody.

**Riana:** What does this mean for me?

**Boss:** You will have to develop new products and start teaching new students.

**Riana:** It doesn't mean more hours?

**Boss:** Not at all. Just more responsibility.

**Riana:** I was told I have to learn a new language.

**Boss:** That is true. We would like you to learn Spanish. However with that comes travel opportunities.

**Riana:** I do like to fly.

**Boss:** You can go by plane or train. Every summer we will have you teach classes for a week on the sea.

**Riana:** That actually sounds incredible.

**Boss:** I think that you will like this promotion.

DIALOGUE 77

# What are you Working on?

**Son:** What are you doing?

**Dad:** Your father is trying to finish his work.

**Son:** Are you drawing? It looks like a ship.

**Dad:** Yes. You know that my job is to design people's homes and this man wants to turn his boat into a home.

**Son:** That's cool. I want to live on a boat too.

**Dad:** For now, we'll stay on land. I like to be on solid ground.

**Son:** Can we at least go on a boat sometime?

**Dad:** Perhaps tomorrow. I think it will be a sunny day.

**Son:** You're the best.

**Dad:** Now you can draw with me if you want, but I have to work for about a half hour more ok?

**Son:** I'll go play some games with my brother.

# Alphabetized List of Words

a
able
about
above
act
add
after
again
against
age
ago
air
all
almost
alone
along
also
always
am
american
among
an
and
animal
another
answer
any
anything
appear
are
area
around
as
ask
at
baby
back
ball
base
be
beauty
because
become
bed
been
before
began
begin
behind
being
below
best
better
between
big
bike
bird
black
blue
boat
body
book
both
bought
box
boy
bring
broke
brother
build
bus
busy
but
buy
by
call
came
can
can't
car
care
carry
cat
cause
center
certain
change
check
children
city
class
clean
clear
close
cold
college
color
come
common
complete
contain
correct
could
country
course
cover
cross
cry
cut
dark
day
decide
deep
develop
did
direct
do
does
dog
done
don't
door
down
draw
drive
dry
during
each
early
earth
ease
east
eat
end
enough
even
ever
every
everything
example
eye
face
fact
fall
family
far
fast
father
favorite
feel
feet
few
field
fight
figure

fill
final
finally
find
fine
fire
first
fish
five
fly
follow
food
foot
for
force
form
found
four
free
friend
from
front
full
funny
game
gave
get
girl
give
go
gold
good
got

great
green
ground
group
grow
had
half
hand
happen
happy
hard
has
have
he
head
hear
heard
heart
heat
help
her
here
high
him
his
history
hold
home
horse
hot
hour
house
how

hundred
idea
if
in
interest
is
island
it
itself
job
just
keep
kind
knew
know
land
language
large
last
late
laugh
lay
lead
learn
leave
left
less
let
letter
life
light
like
line

list
listen
little
live
long
look
lot
love
low
lunch
machine
mad
made
main
make
man
many
map
mark
may
maybe
me
mean
measure
men
might
mile
mind
minute
miss
moment
money
moon

more
morning
most
mother
mountain
move
much
music
must
my
myself
name
near
need
never
new
next
night
no
north
note
nothing
notice
now
number
object
of
off
often
oh
old
on
once

one
only
open
or
order
other
our
out
over
own
page
paper
part
pass
pattern
people
perhaps
person
picture
piece
place
plain
plan
plane
plant
play
point
port
possible
pound
power
press
probably
problem
produce
product
pull
put
question
quick
rain
ran
reach
read
ready
real
recent
record
red
remember
rest
right
river
road
rock
room
round
rule
run
said
same
saw
say
school
science
sea
second
see
seem
self
sentence
serve
set
several
shape
she
ship
short
should
show
side
simple
since
sing
sit
six
size
sleep
slow
small
snow
so
some
something
song
soon
sound
south
special
spell
spirit
stand
star
start
state
stay
step
still
stood
stop
story
street
strong
student
study
such
suddenly
summer
sun
sure
surface
table
tail
take
talk
teach
tell
ten
test
than
that
the
their
them
then
there
these
they
thing
think
this
those
though
thought
thousand
three
through
time
to
together
told
too
took
top
toward
town
train
travel
tree
true
try
turn
two
under
until

| | | | | |
|---|---|---|---|---|
| **up** | **warm** | **well** | **while** | **with** |
| **us** | **was** | **went** | **white** | **without** |
| **use** | **wash** | **were** | **who** | **wonder** |
| **usual** | **watch** | **west** | **whole** | **wood** |
| **very** | **water** | **what** | **why** | **word** |
| **voice** | **way** | **wheel** | **wild** | **work** |
| **wait** | **we** | **when** | **will** | |
| **walk** | **week** | **where** | **wind** | |
| **want** | **weight** | **which** | **winter** | |

# Definitions & Examples

**a** - indefinite article used before singular nouns that start with a consonant sound.

**Example**: I need a pencil.

**able** - having the power or skill to do something.

**Example**: She is able to solve the math problem.

**about** - on the subject of; concerning.

**Example**: We talked about our vacation plans.

**above** - at a higher level or position than something else.

**Example**: The bird flew above the tree.

**act** - take action; do something.

**Example**: He needs to act quickly before it's too late.

**add** - combine two or more quantities to increase the size, number, or amount of something.

**Example**: I need to add sugar to the recipe.

**after** - happening or done later than something else

**Example**: We will meet after lunch.

**again** - one more time; once more.

Example: Let's try again.

**against** - in opposition to; contrary to.

**Example**: I am against the idea of cutting down all the trees in the park.

**age** - the length of time that a person has lived or a thing has existed.

**Example**: Her age is 25 years old.

**ago** - before now; in the past.

**Example**: I saw him two years ago.

**air** - the invisible gaseous substance surrounding the earth, a mixture mainly of oxygen and nitrogen.

**Example**: We need to breathe fresh air to stay healthy.

**all** - the whole quantity or extent of something; every part of something.

**Example**: All of us went to the party.

**almost** - nearly; not quite.

**Example**: I almost missed my flight.

**alone** - on one's own; by oneself.

**Example**: She likes to spend time alone.

**along** - moving in the same direction as; beside.

**Example**: I walked along the riverbank.

**also** - in addition; too.

**Example**: She is talented and also hardworking.

**always** - at all times; on all occasions.

**Example**: She always arrives early for meetings.

**am** - the first-person singular present indicative of the verb to be.

Example: I am a student.

**american** - relating to or characteristic of the United States or its inhabitants.

**Example**: He is an American citizen.

**among** - surrounded by; in the midst of.

**Example**: She felt at home among her friends.

**an** - indefinite article used before singular nouns that start with a vowel sound.

**Example**: He is an engineer.

**and** - a conjunction used to connect words, phrases, or clauses together to indicate that the connected elements belong together in some way.

**Example**: My sister loves to read books and watch movies.

**animal** - a living organism that belongs to the kingdom Animalia and possesses characteristics such as the ability to move, reproduce, and sense its environment.

**Example**: Elephants are one of the largest land animals on the planet.

**another** - an additional or different one of something that has already been mentioned or is known.

**Example**: I already have one blue pen, but I need another one for my class.

**answer** - a solution, explanation, or response to a question or problem.

**Example**: The answer to the math problem is 42.

**any** - used to refer to one or some of a thing or group of things, no matter which or how many.

**Example**: Do you have any pets?

**anything** - any thing, event, or matter, regardless of its nature or importance.

**Example**: I don't have anything planned for the weekend yet.

**appear** - to become visible or present, often suddenly or unexpectedly.

**Example**: The sun will appear in the sky at dawn.

**are** - the second-person singular and plural, and the third-person plural form of the verb be used to indicate present tense.

**Example**: You are the best thing that has ever happened to me.

**area** - a particular part or region of a place, typically one that is defined or marked out.

**Example**: This park has a playground area for children.

**around** - in a circular direction or position, or in the vicinity of a particular place.

**Example**: The restaurant is located around the corner from the movie theater.

**as** - used to introduce a comparison or to indicate the role or function of something.

**Example**: As a teacher, it's important to be patient with students.

**ask** - to inquire about something by requesting information or an answer.

**Example**: I need to ask my boss about taking time off work.

**at** - used to indicate a specific location or place where something is happening or located.

**Example**: The party will be held at my friend's house.

**baby** - a very young human being who is typically under the age of one year

**Example**: The new parents were overjoyed to welcome their baby girl into the world.

**back** - the part of the body that is opposite to the front; also, to return to a previous place or state

**Example**: After carrying the heavy box, she felt a pain in her back.

**ball** - a round object that is typically used in games or sports

**Example**: The kids were playing soccer and kicked the ball back and forth.

**base** - the bottom or foundation of something; also, a place or location where something begins

**Example**: The statue was too heavy, so we had to secure it to the base with bolts.

**be** - to exist or live; also, a word used to indicate the identity or nature of someone or something

**Example**: To be or not to be, that is the question.

**beauty** - the quality or combination of qualities in something that makes it aesthetically pleasing

**Example**: The sunset over the ocean was a display of natural beauty.

**because** - for the reason that; on account of

**Example**: I couldn't go outside because it was raining heavily.

**become** - to come to be; to develop or transform into something else

**Example**: With hard work and dedication, she hopes to become a doctor one day.

**bed** - a piece of furniture used for sleeping or resting on

**Example**: I like to read a book before going to bed.

**been** - past participle of the verb be

**Example**: He had been waiting for her at the coffee shop for over an hour.

**before** - in advance of; earlier than in time; also, in front of

**Example**: She arrived at the party before anyone else.

**began** - past tense of the verb begin

**Example**: The concert began at 8 pm sharp.

**begin** - to start or initiate something

**Example**: She decided to begin her own business after years of working for others.

**behind** - at the back of something or someone; also, in a less advanced position

**Example**: The car behind us honked its horn impatiently.

**being** - a living or existing entity; also, the nature or essence of a person or thing

**Example**: Many people believe in the existence of extraterrestrial beings.

**below** - at a lower level or position; under

**Example**: The basement is located below the ground floor of the house.

**best** - the highest quality or standard; also, the most favorable or desirable option

**Example**: She always strives to do her best in everything she does.

**better** - of a higher or improved quality; also, to improve or surpass something

**Example**: She felt better after taking a nap and drinking some water.

**between** - in the space separating two or more things; also, involving two or more things or people

**Example:** The park is located between the library and the post office.

**big** - of a large size or amount; also, important or significant

**Example:** She received a big promotion at work after years of hard work and dedication.

**bike** - a vehicle with two wheels and pedals that is powered by a person's legs

**Example:** He likes to ride his bike to work instead of driving a car.

**bird** - a warm-blooded vertebrate with feathers, wings, and a beak

**Example:** The robin is a common bird that is often seen in gardens and parks.

**black** - the darkest color, which is the absence of light; also, of the color of coal or the night sky

**Example:** She wore a black dress to the funeral.

**blue** - a color that is similar to the sky or ocean; also, a feeling of sadness or depression

**Example:** The sky was a beautiful shade of blue on a sunny day.

**boat** - a watercraft used for transportation or leisure activities on water

**Example:** They went fishing on a small boat on the lake.

**body** - the physical structure of a person or animal; also, the main part of something

**Example:** She went to the gym to work on strengthening her body.

**book** - a written or printed work that contains information, stories, or other content

**Example:** She loves to read books on a variety of topics, including history and science fiction.

**both** - referring to two things or people together

**Example:** Both John and Jane attended the party last night.

**bought** - past tense of the verb buy, which means to purchase something

**Example:** She bought a new dress for the wedding.

**box** - a container with a flat base and sides, typically used for storing or transporting items

**Example:** She put the old

books in a box and donated them to the library.

**boy** - a male child or young person

**Example**: The boy was playing with his toys in the corner of the room.

**bring** - to carry or convey something to a place or person; also, to cause something to happen

**Example**: She asked her friend to bring some snacks to the party.

**broke** - past tense of the verb break, which means to separate into pieces or cause damage

**Example**: She accidentally broke a glass while washing dishes.

**brother** - a male sibling; also, a close male friend or companion

**Example**: Her brother helped her move into her new apartment.

**build** - to construct or create something; also, to develop or improve something gradually

**Example**: He decided to build a treehouse in his backyard.

**bus** - a large vehicle used for transporting passengers, especially on scheduled routes

**Example**: She takes the bus to work every day instead of driving.

**busy** - actively engaged in a task or activity; also, having a lot of things to do or deal with

**Example**: She was too busy to attend the meeting.

**but** - used to introduce a contrasting statement or idea

**Example**: She wanted to go to the party, but she had to finish her work first.

**buy** - to purchase something with money; also, to acquire something by paying a price for it

**Example**: She decided to buy a new laptop for her work.

**by** - next to or close to something or someone; also, indicating the means or method by which something is done

**Example**: The park is located by the river.

**call** - to communicate with someone by phone, text, or other means; also, to give someone a name or title

**Example**: She called her friend to ask if she wanted to go to the movies.

**came** - past tense of the verb come, which means to move toward or arrive at a particular place

**Example**: She came to the party with her friends.

**can** - to be able to do something; also, a container made of metal or plastic

Example: She can speak three languages fluently.

**can't** - contraction of cannot, which means to be unable to do something

**Example**: She can't attend the meeting due to a scheduling conflict.

**car** - a vehicle with four wheels, typically powered by an internal combustion engine or electric motor

**Example**: She drove her car to work instead of taking the bus.

**care** - to be concerned about or interested in someone or something; also, the provision of what is necessary for the health and well-being of someone or something

**Example**: She takes care of her plants by watering them regularly.

**carry** - to move something from one place to another; also, to support the weight of something or someone

**Example**: She carried the heavy box up the stairs to her apartment.

**cat** - a small domesticated carnivorous mammal with fur, retractable claws, and a distinctive meow

**Example**: She has a black and white cat named Luna.

**cause** - a reason or motive for something; also, to make something happen

**Example**: The heavy rain caused flooding in the streets.

**center** - the middle point or core of something; also, a place or institution that is the focus of a particular activity or interest
**Example**: The city center is the busiest part of town.

**certain** - having no doubt; also, particular but not explicitly named or stated

**Example**: She was certain that she had locked the front door before leaving the house.

**change** - to make or become different; also, money given in exchange for the same amount in a different form

**Example**: She decided to change her hairstyle.

**check** - to examine or inspect something; also, a written order directing a bank to pay money

**Example**: She checked the weather forecast before planning her weekend activities.

**children** - young human beings below the age of puberty; also, offspring of any age

**Example**: She works as a teacher for children with special needs.

**city** - a large town or urban area, typically with a population of over 100,000 people

**Example**: She lives in a bustling city with lots of restaurants and cultural activities.

**class** - a group of students who are taught together; also, a category of things or people

**Example**: She is taking a cooking class at the community center.

**clean** - free from dirt, marks, or unwanted matter; also, to make something free from dirt or unwanted matter

**Example**: She cleaned the kitchen before cooking dinner.

**clear** - easy to see, hear, or understand; also, to remove something that is blocking or obstructing a view

**Example:** She made it clear that she wasn't interested in the job.

**close** - near in space or time; also, to shut or fasten something

**Example**: She lives close to the park.

**cold** - having a low temperature; also, lacking in warmth or affection

**Example**: She put on a sweater because it was cold outside.

**college** - an educational institution that typically provides undergraduate and graduate degrees

**Example**: She attended a liberal arts college in the northeast.

clothes for the trip.

**color** - the property possessed by an object that produces different sensations on the eye as a result of the way it reflects or emits light; also, a pigment or dye used to give something a particular hue

**Example**: She painted her room a bright and cheerful color.

**come** - to move or travel toward a person or place; also, to happen or occur

**Example**: She asked her friend to come over for dinner.

**common** - occurring, found, or done often; also, shared by all members of a group

**Example**: It is common for people to experience jet lag after a long flight.

**complete** - having all necessary parts, elements, or steps; also, to finish or bring something to a conclusion Example: She completed her thesis after months of research and writing.

**contain** - to have something inside or as a part of something else; also, to restrain or control something

**Example:** She packed her suitcase to contain all of her clothes for the trip.

**correct** - free from error or mistake; also, to make something right or accurate

**Example**: She corrected her spelling mistakes before submitting the report.

**could** - past tense of the verb can, which means to be able to do something; also, used to indicate possibility or potential

**Example**: She could have gone to the concert, but she decided not to.

**country** - a nation or state; also, a rural area outside of cities or towns

**Example**: She grew up in a small country town in the Midwest.

**course** - a path or route taken to get to a destination; also, a series of lectures or lessons in a particular subject

**Example:** She signed up for a cooking course at the community college.

**cover** - to place something over or around something else; also, a thing that lies on, over, or around something else

**Example**: She covered the table

with a tablecloth before setting the dinner table.

**cross** - to move or travel from one side of something to another; also, to go against or oppose something

**Example**: She crossed the street carefully to avoid the traffic.

**cry** - to shed tears in response to strong emotion; also, to make a loud, high-pitched sound

**Example**: She cried tears of joy when she found out she got the job.

**cut** - to separate or divide something using a sharp tool or object; also, to reduce or decrease something

**Example**: She cut the cake into equal slices for everyone to enjoy.

**dark** - having little or no light; gloomy or frightening

**Example**: The forest was too dark to navigate without a flashlight.

**day** - a period of 24 hours; the time between sunrise and sunset

**Example**: I spent the entire day at the beach.

**decide** - to make a choice or come to a conclusion after consideration

**Example**: She couldn't decide whether to go to the party or stay home.

**deep** - extending far down from the top or surface; intense or extreme

**Example**: The ocean is very deep and full of mysterious creatures.

**develop** - to grow or cause to grow and become more advanced or mature

**Example**: He has developed a passion for photography over the years.

**did** - past tense of the verb do

**Example**: I did my homework last night.

**direct** - to give instructions or guidance to someone; without an intervening agency or mediator

**Example**: The director will direct the actors during the play.

**do** - to perform an action; to accomplish or complete

**Example**: I need to do my laundry today.

**does** - present tense of the verb do

**Example**: She does her homework every night.

**dog** - a domesticated carnivorous mammal; a common household pet

**Example**: I adopted a new dog from the animal shelter.

**done** - past participle of the verb do

**Example**: The project is done, and it turned out great!

**don't** - contraction of do not

**Example**: Don't forget to bring your umbrella, it's raining outside.

**door** - a movable barrier used to close off an entrance or exit

**Example**: Please close the door when you leave the room.

**down** - toward or in a lower place or position; feeling sad or depressed

**Example**: She felt down after receiving the bad news.

**draw** - to produce a picture or image by making marks on paper or other surface; to attract or pull something closer

**Example**: He likes to draw cartoons in his free time.

**drive** - to operate a vehicle or cause a vehicle to move forward; to motivate or encourage

**Example**: She will drive us to the airport tomorrow morning.

**dry** - lacking moisture; not wet or damp

**Example**: You need to dry your clothes before you wear them.

**during** - throughout the course or duration of a particular time period or event

**Example**: She studied hard during the semester and received good grades.

**each**: every one of two or more people or things considered individually

**Example**: Each student must complete the assignment on their own.

**early**: happening or done before the usual or expected time

**Example**: I woke up early this morning to go for a jog.

**earth**: the planet we live on; the ground or soil

**Example**: The earth orbits around the sun.

**ease**: a state of being comfortable or at ease; to make something easier

**Example**: She reclined on the sofa with ease.

**east**: the direction toward the point of the sunrise; the opposite of west

**Example**: The sun rises in the east and sets in the west.

**eat**: to consume food by mouth

**Example**: I'm hungry, let's eat dinner.

**end**: the final part of something; to bring something to a conclusion

**Example**: The movie had a happy ending.

**enough**: sufficient or adequate in amount or degree

**Example**: I have enough money to buy a new car.

**even**: flat and level; equal or consistent

**Example**: The table was even, with no wobbles.

**ever**: at any time; always

**Example**: Have you ever been to Paris?

**every**: each and all members of a group

**Example**: Every student in the class must pass the exam.

**everything**: all things or all aspects of a situation

**Example**: She packed everything she needed for the trip.

**Example**: a thing characteristic of its kind or illustrating a general rule

**Example**: This painting is a great example of Impressionism.

**eye**: the organ of sight; a small hole or opening

**Example**: She had beautiful blue eyes.

**face**: the front part of the head, with features such as eyes, nose, and mouth

**Example**: She looked at herself

in the mirror and saw her tired face.

**fact**: something that is known or proven to be true

**Example**: The fact that smoking is harmful to health is well-known.

**fall**: to drop or come down from a higher position to a lower one, often suddenly.

**Example**: The leaves fall from the trees in autumn.

**family**: a group consisting of one or two parents and their children living together as a unit

**Example**: I'm going to visit my family this weekend.

**far**: at or to a great distance in space or time

**Example**: We traveled far to see the famous waterfall.

**fast**: moving or able to move quickly

**Example**: He is a fast runner and always wins the race.

**father**: a male parent

**Example**: My father is a doctor.

**favorite**: a person or thing that is preferred over others

**Example**: Pizza is my favorite food.

**feel**: to experience an emotion or sensation; to touch or perceive something

**Example**: I feel happy when I'm with my friends.

**feet:** the lower part of the leg below the ankle, on which a person stands and walks

**Example**: She wore comfortable shoes to ease the pain in her feet.

**few**: a small number of something

**Example**: I have few friends, but they are all very close to me.

**field**: an area of land used for a specific purpose, such as farming or sports

**Example**: The farmers worked in the field to harvest the crops.

**fight**: to engage in physical combat or an argument

**Example**: The two boxers will fight in the championship next week.

**figure**: a shape or outline of a

person or object; a number or symbol

**Example**: The figure skating performance was beautiful to watch.

**fill**: to make something full or complete

**Example**: She filled the glass with water.

**final**: happening or coming at the end of a series

**Example**: This is my final decision on the matter.

**finally**: at last; after a long wait or delay

**Example**: Finally, the train arrived at the station.

**find**: to discover or locate something that was previously lost or unknown

**Example**: I was able to find my lost keys in the sofa cushions.

**fine**: good or satisfactory; a penalty for breaking a law or rule

**Example**: The weather is fine today, let's go for a walk.

**fire**: a combustion process that produces heat and light; a state of burning

**Example**: The fire in the fireplace kept us warm all night.

**first**: coming before all others in time or order

**Example**: I was the first to arrive at the party.

**fish**: a cold-blooded aquatic animal with scales, gills, and fins

**Example**: We went fishing at the lake and caught a lot of fish.

**five**: the number equivalent to the quantity of fingers on one hand

**Example**: There are five people in my family.

**fly**: to move through the air with wings

**Example**: The bird flew away when it saw us approaching.

**follow**: to go or come after someone or something

**Example**: I will follow you wherever you go.

**food**: any substance that is consumed in order to provide nutritional support for the body

**Example**: I love to eat Italian

food, especially pasta.

**foot**: the lower part of the leg below the ankle, on which a person stands and walks

**Example**: She kicked the ball with her foot.

**for**: used to indicate the recipient or beneficiary of an action or the purpose or reason for something

**Example**: She bought flowers for her mother's birthday.

**force**: strength or energy exerted or brought to bear, typically causing an action or movement

**Example**: The strong wind force caused the trees to sway.

**form**: the visible shape or configuration of something

**Example**: The sculpture has a unique form.

**found**: to establish or originate something

**Example**: She founded the company ten years ago.

**four**: the number equivalent to the quantity of fingers on one hand plus one

**Example**: I have four siblings.

**free**: not subject to payment or having restrictions

**Example**: The museum offers free admission on Sundays.

**friend**: a person whom one knows and with whom one has a bond of mutual affection

**Example**: I have many good friends from college.

**from**: indicating the point in space or time at which a journey, motion, or action starts

**Example**: The train is coming from the north.

**front**: the part or side of something that faces forward or is most often seen or used

**Example**: She sat at the front of the class.

**full**: having all the necessary or typical parts or components; containing as much or as many as possible

**Example**: The bottle is full of water.

**funny**: causing laughter or amusement; humorous

**Example**: The comedian told a

funny joke.

**game**: an activity or sport that has rules and is played for entertainment or competition

**Example**: The children played a game of hide and seek.

**gave**: past tense of give, to transfer possession of something to someone else as a gift or payment

**Example**: She gave me a birthday present.

**get**: to obtain, acquire or receive something

**Example**: I need to get some milk from the grocery store.

**girl**: a female child or young woman

**Example**: The girl was playing with her doll.

**give**: to transfer possession of something to someone else as a gift or payment

**Example**: Can you give me a hand with this heavy box?

**go**: to move from one place to another; to leave or depart

**Example**: We need to go to the grocery store to buy some food.

**gold**: a precious metal that is yellow in color and is used for jewelry and currency

**Example**: The Olympic medals are made of gold, silver, and bronze.

**good**: of high quality or excellent standard; morally right or righteous

**Example**: She did a good job on her project.

**got**: past tense of get, to obtain, acquire or receive something

**Example**: I got a new job last week.

**great**: of an extent, amount, or intensity considerably above the normal or average

**Example**: The concert was great, and the audience was cheering all night.

**green**: a color that is a mixture of yellow and blue; relating to or being concerned with conservation of the environment

**Example**: The grass is green in the park.

**ground**: the solid surface of the earth; an area of land used for a particular purpose

**Example**: The coffee beans are ground into a fine powder.

**group**: a number of people or things that are located, gathered or classed together

**Example**: We formed a study group to prepare for the exam.

**grow**: to increase in size, amount or extent; to develop or become mature

**Example**: The flowers are growing in the garden.

**had**: past tense of have, to possess, own or hold something

**Example**: She had a lot of work to do yesterday.

**half**: one of two equal or nearly equal parts into which something can be divided

**Example**: I ate only half of my sandwich.

**hand**: the end part of an arm, beyond the wrist, that is used for holding, touching, or manipulating objects

**Example**: She washed her hands before eating.

**happen**: to occur, take place, or come to pass

**Example**: I don't know what will happen in the future.

**happy**: feeling or showing pleasure or contentment

**Example**: I am very happy to see you.

**hard**: requiring great effort or endurance; difficult or challenging

**Example**: It was a hard climb to the top of the mountain.

**has**: present tense of have, to possess, own or hold something

**Example**: She has a new car.

**have**: to possess, own or hold something

**Example**: I have a meeting at noon.

**he**: used to refer to a male person or animal that has already been mentioned or is easily identified

**Example**: He is my brother.

**head**: the upper part of the body, which contains the brain, eyes, mouth, and nose

**Example**: She shook her head

to indicate that she disagreed.

**hear**: to perceive with the ear; to be told or informed of something

**Example**: Can you hear the music playing in the background?

**heard**: past tense of hear, to perceive with the ear; to be told or informed of something

**Example**: She heard a noise outside her window.

**heart**: the organ in the chest that pumps blood throughout the body; the center of a person's thoughts, emotions, and personality

**Example**: She felt her heart pounding with excitement.

**heat**: the quality of being hot; a form of energy that causes things to become warmer

**Example**: I turned up the heat to warm the room.

**help**: to give assistance or support; to make it easier or possible for someone to do something

**Example**: Can you help me carry these boxes?

**her**: used to refer to a female person or animal that has already been mentioned or is easily identified

**Example**: Her name is Sarah.

**here**: in, at, or to this place or position

**Example**: I am here to meet with you.

**high**: having a great vertical extent or distance from the bottom to the top; being above the usual or average level

**Example**: The airplane flew at a high altitude.

**him**: used to refer to a male person or animal that has already been mentioned or is easily identified

**Example**: I gave him a book as a present.

**his**: belonging to or associated with a male person or animal that has already been mentioned or is easily identified

**Example**: His car is parked outside.

**history**: the study of past events, particularly in human affairs; a chronological record of significant events in the past

**Example**: She is studying history at university.

**hold**: to have and keep in one's grasp; to support or sustain something in a particular position or state

**Example**: She held the baby in her arms.

**home**: the place where one lives permanently, especially as a member of a family or household; a place of origin or belonging

**Example**: He went home after work.

**horse**: a large four-legged mammal, often used for riding or for pulling carts and carriages

**Example**: She rode a horse in the countryside.

**hot**: having a high degree of heat; spicy or pungent in flavor.

**Example**: The soup was too hot for me to eat.

**hour**: a period of time consisting of 60 minutes; a particular point in time

**Example**: We had a meeting at two o'clock in the afternoon.

**house**: a building for human habitation, especially one that is lived in by a family or small group of people

**Example**: They bought a new house in the suburbs.

**how**: in what way or manner; to what extent or degree

**Example**: How are you feeling today?

**hundred**: the number equivalent to the product of ten and ten; a large but unspecified number

**Example**: He counted to one hundred.

**idea**: a thought or concept that exists in the mind, often resulting in plans or actions

**Example**: She had a great idea for a new business.

**if**: a conjunction used to indicate a possibility or hypothetical situation

**Example**: If it rains, we'll stay indoors.

**in**: located inside or within something; expressing the time during which an event occurs

**Example**: She left her keys in the car.

**interest**: a feeling of curiosity or concern about something; the state of wanting to know more about something; the quality of being important or relevant

**Example**: I have an interest in learning new languages.

**is**: a form of to be indicating present tense, used to identify or describe something

**Example**: The sky is blue.

**island**: a piece of land surrounded by water on all sides

**Example**: They went on a vacation to a tropical island.

**it**: used to refer to a thing previously mentioned or easily identified

**Example**: The book was on the shelf, and she picked it up.

**itself**: used to emphasize a noun or pronoun as the object of a verb or preposition

**Example**: The cat licked itself clean.

**job**: a task or piece of work that someone is responsible for; a paid position of regular employment

**Example**: She applied for a job at the local library.

**just**: exactly or precisely; based on what is morally or ethically right

**Example**: She wanted to be treated justly.

**keep**: to have or retain possession of something; to maintain something in a particular state or condition

**Example**: She kept her jewelry in a safe.

**kind**: a type or category of something; having a generous, helpful, or caring nature

**Example**: He was always kind to animals.

**knew**: past tense of know, to have information about something in one's mind

**Example**: She knew the answer to the question.

**know**: to have information about something in one's mind; to be familiar or acquainted with something or someone

**Example**: Do you know the way to the train station?

**land**: the solid ground or

surface of the earth; an area of ground, especially when used for a particular purpose

**Example**: They bought a piece of land to build their dream home on.

**language**: the method of communication used by a particular community or country; a system of words or symbols used to represent ideas

**Example**: She is fluent in several languages, including Spanish and French.

**large**: of considerable or relatively great size, extent, or capacity

**Example**: They moved into a large house in the suburbs.

**last**: coming after all others in time or order; the final one

**Example**: She was the last person to leave the party.

**late**: occurring or being done after the expected or usual time; near the end of a period of time

**Example**: She arrived late for her meeting.

**laugh**: to make sounds with the voice, expressing amusement or pleasure; to find something amusing or funny

**Example**: The comedian made the audience laugh with his jokes.

**lay**: to put something in a particular position, especially carefully or for a particular purpose; to recline

**Example**: She laid the book on the table.

**lead**: to show the way; to guide or direct others; a metal that is very dense and soft

**Example**: She led the group on a hike through the forest.

**learn**: to acquire knowledge or skills through study or experience; to gain information

**Example**: He is learning to play the guitar.

**leave**: to go away from a place; to allow someone or something to remain behind

**Example**: She is leaving for vacation tomorrow.

**left**: the opposite of right; remaining after everything else has gone

**Example**: She turned left at the intersection.

**less**: a smaller amount of something; not as much as before

**Example**: She had less time to complete the task than she had expected.

**let**: to allow someone or something to do something; to rent or lease a property

**Example**: She let her dog run in the park.

**letter**: a written or printed communication addressed to a person or organization

**Example**: She received a letter from her friend who was traveling abroad.

**life**: the existence of an individual, animal, or plant; the condition that distinguishes living things from non-living things

**Example**: She enjoys spending time outdoors and experiencing the beauty of life.

**light**: the natural agent that stimulates sight and makes things visible; having little weight; not heavy

**Example**: She turned on the light in the room.

**like**: having the same characteristics or qualities as something; enjoying or finding something pleasing

**Example**: She likes to read books in her spare time.

**line**: a long, narrow mark or band; a row of people or things

**Example**: She waited in line for her turn.

**list**: a number of connected items or names written or printed consecutively, usually one below the other

**Example**: She made a list of the things she needed to buy at the grocery store.

**listen**: to give attention to sound; to hear something and take notice of it

**Example**: She likes to listen to music while she works.

**little**: small in size, amount, or degree; not much

**Example**: She has a little bit of sugar in her coffee.

**live**: to exist or be alive; to reside in a particular place

**Example**: She lives in a small

apartment in the city.

**long**: having a great distance from one end to the other; lasting for a considerable time

**Example**: She went on a long hike through the mountains.

**look**: to direct one's gaze in a particular direction; to appear or seem

**Example**: She looked out the window and saw the sunset.

**lot**: a large number or amount; a portion of land

**Example**: She bought a lot of groceries at the store.

**love**: a strong feeling of affection or attachment towards someone or something; an intense emotional attachment

**Example**: She fell in love with him the moment she met him.

**low**: situated close to the ground or the bottom; not high or tall; having a small or reduced quantity or level

**Example**: The temperature is quite low today.

**lunch**: a meal eaten in the middle of the day, typically consisting of a light or informal fare

**Example**: She packed a sandwich for her lunch.

**machine**: a mechanical or electronic device that performs a specific function

**Example**: The factory has installed new machines to increase productivity.

**mad**: feeling or showing anger, resentment, or extreme emotion

**Example**: He was mad when he found out he didn't get the job he had applied for.

**made**: produced, created, or manufactured by a person or machine

**Example**: She made a beautiful dress for her daughter's wedding.

**main**: most important, principal, or leading

**Example**: The main reason for the delay was due to bad weather.

**make**: to create or produce something; to cause something to happen

**Example**: She's going to make dinner for us tonight.

**man**: an adult human male

**Example**: The man standing over there is my uncle.

**many**: a large number of something

**Example**: There were many people at the concert last night.

**map**: a diagrammatic representation of an area of land or sea showing physical features, cities, roads, etc.

**Example**: He studied the map carefully to find the best route.

**mark**: a visible impression or trace on something, such as a stain or a scar; a symbol or sign that represents something

**Example**: She put a mark on the page where she left off reading.

**may**: expressing possibility or permission

**Example**: May I borrow your pen for a moment?

**maybe**: perhaps; possibly

**Example**: Maybe we should go to the park today.

**me**: used to refer to the speaker or writer

**Example**: Can you hear me?

**mean**: to intend to express or convey something; to have as a purpose or intention

**Example**: I didn't mean to hurt your feelings.

**measure**: to determine the size, amount, or degree of something using an instrument or standard

**Example**: She measured the length of the room to see if the couch would fit.

**men**: plural form of man, referring to adult human males

**Example**: The men in the office were all dressed in suits.

**might**: used to indicate possibility or uncertainty

**Example**: She might come to the party, but she hasn't decided yet.

**mile**: a unit of length equal to 5,280 feet or 1.609 kilometers

**Example**: The marathon is 26.2 miles long.

**mind**: the faculty of consciousness and thought; the mental or psychological aspect of a person

**Example**: She couldn't get him out of her mind all day.

**minute**: a period of time equal to sixty seconds; a short space of time

**Example**: She only had a few minutes to catch the bus.

**miss**: to fail to hit, catch, or reach something; to feel the absence of someone or something

**Example**: She always misses her family when she's away from home.

**moment**: a very brief period of time; a particular time or occasion

**Example**: She had a moment of clarity and realized what she needed to do.

**money**: a medium of exchange in the form of coins, banknotes, or digital transactions, used to purchase goods or services

**Example**: I need to withdraw some money from the ATM before we go shopping.

**moon**: the natural satellite of the Earth, visible at night as a bright object in the sky

**Example**: They watched the moon rise over the horizon.

**more**: a greater or additional amount or degree of something

**Example**: He wanted more cake after he finished his first piece.

**morning**: the period of time between midnight and noon; the first part of the day

**Example**: She likes to go for a walk every morning before work.

**most**: the majority or greatest number of something; to the greatest extent or degree

**Example**: Most people prefer coffee over tea.

**mother**: a female parent; a woman in authority

**Example**: She called her mother to wish her a happy birthday.

**mountain**: a large natural elevation of the Earth's surface, rising steeply from the surrounding area

**Example**: They went hiking in the mountains last weekend.

**move**: to change position or location; to cause something to change position or location

**Example**: He helped his friend move to a new apartment.

**much**: a large quantity or amount of something; to a great extent

**Example**: She ate too much pizza and felt sick.

**music**: the art of sound in time that expresses ideas and emotions through the elements of rhythm, melody, harmony, and timbre

**Example**: He loves to listen to classical music when he's working.

**must**: used to indicate that something is highly recommended or necessary; used to express a strong opinion or determination

**Example**: You must see that movie, it's amazing.

**my**: belonging to or associated with the speaker or writer

**Example**: My favorite color is blue.

**myself**: used to refer to the speaker or writer as the object of a verb or preposition, for emphasis or clarity

**Example**: I made the decision myself, no one else helped me.

**name**: a word or set of words by which a person, animal, place, or thing is known, addressed, or referred to

**Example**: My name is John.

**near**: at or to a short distance away; close in space or time

**Example**: The store is near the park.

**need**: require something because it is essential or very important

**Example**: I need to buy groceries for the week.

**never**: at no time in the past or future; not ever

**Example**: She has never been to Europe.

**new**: not existing before; recently made or created

**Example**: I bought a new car last week.

**next**: coming immediately after the present time or event; the one after the present one

**Example**: I have a meeting next Tuesday.

**night**: the period of darkness in each twenty-four hours; the time from sunset to sunrise

**Example**: She enjoys reading a book before bed every night.

**no**: not any; used to give a negative response or to express disagreement

**Example**: No, I haven't seen that movie.

**north**: the direction towards the point on the horizon that is directly opposite to south

**Example**: Canada is located north of the United States.

**note**: a brief record of something written down to assist the memory or for future reference

**Example**: I took a note of the important points from the meeting.

**nothing**: not anything; no single thing

**Example**: There was nothing left in the fridge to eat.

**notice**: to observe or become aware of something; a written or printed announcement

**Example**: I noticed the sign on the door that said Closed.

**now**: at the present time or moment; immediately

**Example**: I am currently studying for my exams right now.

**number**: a quantity or value expressed in figures; a numeral or group of numerals

**Example**: The phone number for the restaurant is on their website.

**object**: a material thing that can be seen and touched; a goal or purpose

**Example**: The object on the shelf caught my eye.

**of**: expressing the relationship between a part and a whole; indicating the material or substance used

**Example**: The pages of the book were yellowed with age.

**off**: away from a place; no longer in contact with something

**Example**: He took the hat off his

head.

**often**: frequently; many times

**Example**: I often take walks in the park.

**oh**: used to express a range of emotions including surprise, excitement, or disappointment

**Example**: Oh no, I left my phone at home.

**old**: having lived for a long time; no longer young

**Example**: My grandmother is 95 years old.

**on**: physically in contact with and supported by a surface; indicating a state of being in operation or in progress

**Example**: The book is on the table.

**once**: one time only; at some time in the past

**Example**: I once visited Paris.

**one**: the number equivalent to the Roman numeral I; used to refer to a person or thing previously mentioned or easily identified

**Example**: Can I have one cookie, please?

**only**: no more than; exclusively; merely

**Example**: He was the only person in the room.

open: allowing access, passage, or view; not closed or blocked

**Example**: The door to the room was open.

**or**: used to link alternatives

**Example**: Would you like tea or coffee?

**order**: a request or instruction for something to be made, supplied, or served; a particular arrangement or sequence

**Example**: I placed an order for a pizza.

**other**: used to refer to a person or thing different or distinct from one already mentioned or known

**Example**: The other day, I saw a bird in the garden.

**our**: belonging to or associated with us

**Example**: Our house is on the corner of the street.

**out**: away from the inside or

center; no longer alight or burning

**Example**: She went out for a walk.

**over**: extending directly upward from; finished; in excess of

**Example**: The bridge spans over the river.

**own**: belonging to oneself or itself

**Example**: I have my own apartment.

**page**: one side of a sheet of paper in a book, magazine, or newspaper; a website on the internet

**Example**: I turned the page to continue reading the novel.

**paper**: material manufactured in thin sheets from the pulp of wood or other fibrous substances; a newspaper or magazine

**Example**: I wrote the letter on a piece of paper.

**part**: a piece or section of something larger; a role or character played by an actor

**Example**: The car engine is made up of many different parts.

**pass**: move in a specified direction; transfer something to someone; succeed in an examination or test

**Example**: I passed the ball to my teammate.

**pattern**: a repeated decorative design; a regular or discernible form or order in which something occurs or is done

**Example**: The wallpaper had a floral pattern.

**people**: human beings in general or considered collectively; a community of persons sharing a common culture, history, or language

**Example**: The people of this town are very friendly.

**perhaps**: used to express uncertainty or possibility

**Example**: Perhaps we should wait until the rain stops before going outside.

**person**: a human being regarded as an individual; a figure in grammar representing one or more individuals

**Example**: I met a very interesting person at the party.

**picture**: a painting, drawing, or photograph; a graphic representation of something

**Example**: I hung a picture of my family on the wall.

**piece**: a portion or part of something larger; a work of art, literature, or music

**Example**: She ate a piece of cake for dessert.

**place**: a particular position or location; a building or area used for a particular purpose

**Example**: We found a nice place to have a picnic in the park.

**plain**: not decorated or elaborate; lacking beauty or excitement; a large area of flat land

**Example**: The walls of the room were painted plain white.

**plan**: a detailed proposal for doing or achieving something; a scheme or program

**Example**: We need to come up with a plan for our next vacation.

**plane**: a flat surface; an aircraft

**Example**: The plane took off from the runway.

**plant**: a living organism typically growing in soil; a factory or industrial installation

**Example**: I watered the plants in the garden.

**play**: engage in activity for enjoyment or recreation; a dramatic work for the stage or to be broadcast on radio or television

**Example**: The children were playing in the park.

**point**: a specific location or position in space or time.

**Example**: The point where the two lines intersect is called the point of intersection.

**port**: a place on the coast or by a river where ships can load and unload goods.

**Example**: The largest port in the United States is the Port of South Louisiana.

**possible**: capable of happening or being done.

**Example**: It's possible that it will rain tomorrow, so you should bring an umbrella just in case.

**pound**: a unit of weight equal to

16 ounces or 0.4536 kilograms. **Example**: The recipe calls for two pounds of flour.

**power**: the ability or capacity to do something.

**Example**: Solar panels have the power to generate electricity from sunlight.

**press**: to push against something with force. Example: She had to press hard on the button to make the elevator doors close.

**probably**: likely to happen or be true.

**Example**: He will probably be late because he always gets stuck in traffic on this road.

**problem**: a matter or situation that needs to be dealt with and solved.

**Example**: The biggest problem with this plan is that we don't have enough funding to make it happen.

**produce**: to create or make something.

**Example**: This factory produces over a thousand cars every day.

**product**: something that is made or created as a result of a process. Example: The new product line includes a variety of skincare items.

**pull**: to use force to move something towards you.

**Example**: She had to pull hard to open the door because it was stuck.

**put**: to place something in a particular position or location.

**Example**: Can you please put the book back on the shelf when you're finished reading it?

**question**: an inquiry or request for information.

**Example**: Can you answer my question about the homework assignment?

**quick**: happening or done with great speed or efficiency.

**Example**: She was quick to finish her work and went for a run afterward.

**rain**: precipitation in the form of water droplets falling from the sky.

**Example**: It's raining outside, so I need to bring an umbrella.

**ran**: past tense of the verb run, meaning to move at a quick pace using your feet.

**Example**: He ran a marathon last year and finished in under four hours.

**reach**: to arrive at or attain a particular place, level, or condition.

**Example**: If you keep studying, you'll reach your academic goals.

**read**: to look at and comprehend the meaning of written or printed matter.

**Example**: She loves to read books before going to bed.

**ready**: prepared or in a suitable state for immediate use or action.

**Example**: I'm ready to go on vacation and have my suitcase packed.

**real**: actually existing as a thing or occurring in fact; not imagined or supposed.

**Example:** The pain she felt was real, not just in her mind.

**recent**: happening or occurring not long ago; belonging to a past period of time close to the present.

**Example**: I saw her at the grocery store recently, and she looked happy.

**record**: a written or stored account of something that has happened, particularly in the form of data or information.

**Example**: The world record for the 100-meter dash was broken yesterday.

**red**: a color resembling the hue of blood or fire.

**Example**: The apple she picked from the tree was bright red and juicy.

**remember**: to recall information from memory; to not forget.
**Example**: Can you remember where you left your keys this morning?

**rest**: a period of relaxation or inactivity.

**Example:** After a long day of work, she was looking forward to getting some rest.

**right**: correct or accurate; in accordance with what is just, lawful, or morally right.

**Example**: She made the right decision to apologize for her mistake.

**river**: a large natural stream of water that flows towards the sea, a lake, or another river.

**Example:** The Amazon River is the second-longest river in the world.

**road**: a wide way leading from one place to another, especially one with a specially prepared surface that vehicles can use.

**Example**: We drove on the winding road to reach the top of the mountain.

rock: a naturally occurring **solid** substance composed of minerals and/or organic materials.

**Example**: She climbed up the rocky trail to reach the summit of the hill.

**room**: a space that is or may be occupied by a person or people for a particular purpose.

**Example**: We need to clean the living room before our guests arrive.

**round**: shaped like or approximately like a circle or sphere.

**Example**: The moon is a round celestial body that orbits around the Earth.

**rule**: a principle that governs behavior or actions; an official instruction or order.

**Example:** In order to maintain order, we need to follow the rules of the game.

**run**: to move quickly on foot, particularly for a long distance or period of time.

**Example**: She likes to run every morning to stay in shape.

**said**: past tense of the verb say, meaning to speak or utter words.

**Example**: He said that he would be late for the meeting.

**same**: identical or not different; not changed or modified.

**Example**: We have the same taste in music and often listen to the same songs.

**saw**: a tool with a long, serrated blade used for cutting wood or other materials.

**Example**: He used a saw to cut the piece of wood into smaller pieces.

**say**: to utter words; to express something in speech or writing.

**Example**: She wanted to say something, but she was too nervous to speak.

**school**: an educational institution where students learn academic subjects and receive formal education.

**Example**: She attends a private school in the city and studies various subjects.

**science**: a systematic and logical approach to discovering knowledge about the natural world through experimentation and observation.

**Example**: Biology and chemistry are examples of science subjects studied in school.

**sea**: a large body of saltwater that covers most of the Earth's surface and is home to diverse marine life.

**Example**: She went on a vacation to a tropical island and enjoyed swimming in the sea.

**second**: the unit of time equal to one sixtieth of a minute.

**Example**: He finished the race in second place, just a fraction of a second behind the winner.

**see**: to perceive or become aware of something by using one's eyes.

**Example**: She saw a beautiful sunset while walking on the beach.

**seem**: to give the impression of being or having a particular quality or characteristic.

**Example**: It seems like it's going to rain, so we should bring an umbrella.

**self**: the individual as the object of introspection or reflexive action.

**Example**: She believes in the importance of self-care to maintain mental and physical health.

**sentence**: a grammatically complete series of words that express a complete thought or idea.

**Example**: She wrote a complex sentence in her essay, demonstrating her strong writing skills.

**serve**: to perform duties or fulfill a role for someone or something.

**Example**: She volunteers at a local soup kitchen to serve meals to the homeless.

**set**: to put or place something in a particular position or arrangement.

**Example**: She set the table for dinner with plates, silverware, and glasses.

**several**: more than two but not many; some or a few.

**Example**: Several people showed up to the party, but it wasn't too crowded.

**shape**: the external form or appearance of something.

**Example**: She worked out regularly to maintain her physical shape and fitness.

**she**: a pronoun used to refer to a female person or animal.

**Example**: She is my best friend, and we enjoy spending time together.

**ship**: a large seafaring vessel that transports goods or people across water.

**Example**: The cargo ship docked at the port to unload its cargo.

**short**: of a small length or distance; not tall or long.

**Example**: She wore a short dress to the party and paired it with high heels.

**should**: used to indicate a recommendation or what is considered right or appropriate.

**Example**: You should study for your exams if you want to do well.

**show**: to display or exhibit something to an audience.

**Example**: She decided to show her artwork at a local gallery to get exposure.

**side**: one of the two or more parts of something that are furthest from the center.

**Example**: She prefers to sleep on her right side, as it is more comfortable.

**simple**: easy to understand or do; uncomplicated or straightforward.

**Example**: The recipe for this dish is simple, requiring only a few ingredients.

**since**: from a particular point in time or event until the present or another specified time.

**Example**: She has been studying English since she was in elementary school.

**sing**: to make musical sounds with the voice; to perform or produce music using the voice.

**Example**: She loves to sing and

performs in a local choir.

**sit**: to be seated or in a position where the weight of the body is supported by a chair, the ground, or another surface.

**Example**: She likes to sit by the window and read a book while drinking her coffee.

**six**: the number that comes after five and before seven.

**Example**: She has six siblings, and they often spend time together as a family.

**size**: the dimensions or magnitude of something, typically in terms of length, width, or height.

**Example**: She tried on a dress in a size medium but found that it was too small.

**sleep**: the natural state of rest that occurs during periods of inactivity, typically at night.

**Example**: She had trouble falling asleep due to stress and anxiety.

**slow**: not moving or operating quickly; taking a comparatively long time.

**Example**: She walks at a slow pace, enjoying the scenery around her.

**small**: of a size that is less than normal or usual; little.

**Example**: She bought a small cake for her friend's birthday party as they were only a few guests.

**snow**: atmospheric water vapor that freezes and falls to the ground as ice crystals or snowflakes.

**Example**: She loves to ski in the winter and enjoys the fresh snow on the slopes.

**so:** to such a great extent or degree; used to connect clauses or sentences expressing result or consequence.

**Example**: She was so tired after a long day at work that she fell asleep immediately.

**some**: an unspecified amount or number of something; a few or several.

**Example**: She bought some groceries on her way home from work.

**something**: a thing that is unspecified or unknown; an object, action, or idea.

**Example**: She felt like she

forgot something important but couldn't remember what it was.

**song**: a musical composition that is sung, typically with lyrics.

**Example**: She enjoys listening to pop songs on the radio while driving.

**soon**: in a short time; before long; in the near future.

**Example**: She promised to finish the project soon and submit it to her boss.

**sound**: vibrations that travel through the air and can be heard when they reach a person's ear.

**Example**: She loves the sound of birds singing in the morning.

**south**: the direction toward the point of the horizon 90 degrees clockwise from east, or the opposite direction to north.

**Example**: She is planning to travel south for her vacation to enjoy the warm weather.

**special**: better, greater, or otherwise different from what is usual or ordinary.

**Example**: She cooked a special meal for her parents' anniversary.

**spell**: to form words correctly by writing or speaking them in the correct order.

**Example**: She had to spell her name for the receptionist to find her appointment.

**spirit**: the non-physical part of a person that is believed to give life to the body and to represent a person's thoughts and feelings.

**Example**: She felt a warm spirit of generosity when her friend gave her a gift.

**stand**: to be on one's feet; to support oneself in an upright position.

**Example**: She had to stand in line for hours to get tickets to the concert.

**star**: a luminous celestial body that is visible in the night sky.

**Example**: She loves to stargaze on clear nights to see the constellations.

**start**: to begin or commence an action or process.

**Example**: She decided to start a new hobby and began taking painting classes.

**state**: a nation or territory considered as an organized

political community under one government.

**Example**: She was born and raised in the state of California.

**stay**: to remain in a particular place or position; to continue to be in a particular state or condition.

**Example**: She decided to stay home and read a book instead of going out with her friends.

**step**: a movement made by lifting one foot and putting it down in a different place.

**Example**: She took a step forward to get a better look at the painting.

**still**: not moving or making a sound; calm and tranquil.

**Example**: She sat still and listened to the quiet of the forest.

**stood**: to be in an upright position on one's feet.

**Example**: She stood in front of the mirror and practiced her speech.

**stop**: to come to an end; to cease or halt an action or process.

**Example**: She had to stop working on her project and take a break.

**story**: an account of imaginary or real people and events told for entertainment or education.

**Example**: She loves to read and write stories about fantasy worlds.

**street**: a public road in a town or city, typically with houses and buildings on one or both sides.

**Example**: She lives on a quiet street with little traffic and enjoys taking walks in the evening.

**strong**: having the power to move heavy weights or perform other physically demanding tasks.

**Example**: She works out at the gym to keep her muscles strong.

**student**: a person who is studying at a school or university.

**Example**: She is a full-time student studying engineering at a university.

**study**: the act of learning about a subject through reading, researching, or attending classes.

**Example**: She spends several hours each day studying for her exams.

**such**: of the type previously mentioned or easily identified; of a kind that; like the one or ones already mentioned or implied.

**Example**: She loves to travel to exotic locations, such as Bali or Thailand.

**suddenly**: happening quickly and unexpectedly.

**Example**: She was walking down the street when suddenly it started to rain.

**summer**: the warmest season of the year, between spring and autumn.

**Example**: She loves to go to the beach in the summer and soak up the sun.

**sun**: the star that is the central body of the solar system, around which the planets revolve and from which they receive light and heat.

**Example**: She likes to sit outside in the sun and read a book.

**sure**: confident in what one thinks or knows; having no doubt.

**Example**: She was sure she had locked the door before leaving the house.

**surface**: the outermost or uppermost layer of something; the outside part or appearance of something.

**Example**: She wiped the surface of the table clean before setting the dishes on it.

**table**: a piece of furniture with a flat top and one or more legs.

**Example**: She sat at the table and ate breakfast with her family.

**tail**: the hindmost part of an animal, especially when prolonged beyond the rest of the body..

**Example**: She saw a cat with a long, bushy tail wandering through the garden.

**take**: to lay hold of (something) with one's hands; to pick up and move or remove.

**Example**: She decided to take a vacation to a tropical island for some relaxation.

**talk**: to speak in order to give information or express ideas or feelings; to converse or communicate with someone.

**Example**: She enjoys having long talks with her friends about their lives and experiences.

**teach**: to impart knowledge or skill to someone through instruction or example.

**Example**: She loves to teach children how to read and write in her spare time.

**tell**: to communicate information, facts, or news to someone; to reveal or disclose.

**Example**: She told her friend the good news about her job promotion.

**ten**: a number equivalent to the product of five and two; one more than nine.

**Example**: She counted to ten before jumping into the pool.

**test**: a procedure intended to establish the quality, performance, or reliability of something, especially before it is taken into widespread use.

**Example**: She has to take a test in math tomorrow to measure her understanding of algebra.

**than**: introducing the second element in a comparison; used to introduce an exception or contrast.

**Example**: She is taller than her younger sister, but not as tall as her older brother.

**that**: used to identify a specific person or thing observed or heard by the speaker.

**Example**: She saw that bird sitting on the tree branch.

**the**: denoting one or more people or things already mentioned or assumed to be common knowledge.

**Example**: She went to the store to buy the groceries she needed for the week.

**their**: belonging to or associated with the people or things previously mentioned or easily identified.

**Example**: She saw her neighbors walking their dogs in the park.

**them**: used as the object of a verb or preposition to refer to two or more people or things previously mentioned or easily identified.

**Example**: She gave them the books they needed for their project.

**then**: at that time; immediately afterward.

**Example**: She finished her homework, then went outside to play.

**there**: in, at, or to that place or position.

**Example**: She put her keys down over there on the table.

**these**: used to identify a specific person or thing close at hand or being indicated or experienced.

**Example**: She tried on these shoes and decided they fit perfectly.

**they**: used to refer to two or more people or things previously mentioned or easily identified.

**Example**: She asked her coworkers if they wanted to grab lunch together.

**thing**: an object that one need not, cannot, or does not wish to give a specific name to.

**Example**: She found a thing in her closet that she thought she had lost.

**think**: have a particular belief or idea about something; use one's mind actively to form connected ideas.

**Example**: She thinks that exercising regularly is important for staying healthy.

**this**: used to identify a specific person or thing close at hand or being indicated or experienced.

**Example**: She picked up this book and started reading the first chapter.

**those**: used to identify a specific person or thing at a distance from both speaker and listener or being indicated or experienced.

**Example**: She pointed at those mountains in the distance and said she wanted to hike there someday.

**though**: despite the fact that; however.

**Example**: She decided to go to the party though she was feeling tired.

**thought**: an idea or opinion produced by thinking, or occurring suddenly in the mind.
**Example**: She had a thought that maybe she should call her friend and check in on her.

**thousand**: the number equivalent to the product of a hundred and ten; 1,000.

**Example**: She counted up to a thousand before giving up.

**three**: equivalent to the sum of one and two; one more than two, or half of six.

**Example**: She has three dogs as pets.

**through**: moving in one side and out of the other side of (an opening, channel, or location).

**Example**: She walked through the park to get to her friend's house.

**time**: the indefinite continued progress of existence and events in the past, present, and future regarded as a whole.

**Example:** She spends a lot of time reading books.

**to**: expressing motion in the direction of (a particular location).

**Example**: She went to the store to buy some groceries.

**together**: with or in proximity to another person or people.

**Example**: She and her friends went to the concert together.

**told**: say something to someone, typically in a solemn and emotional way.

**Example**: She told her friend that she appreciated their support.

**too**: to a higher degree than is desirable, permissible, or possible; excessively.

**Example**: She ate too much food at the party and felt sick afterward.

**took**: past tense of the verb take, meaning to lay hold of (something) with one's hands; reach for and hold.

**Example**: She took the book from the shelf and started reading.

**top**: the highest or uppermost point, part, or surface of something.

**Example**: She put the vase on top of the table.

**toward**: in the direction of.

**Example**: She walked toward the bus stop to catch the next bus.

**town**: a built-up area with a name, defined boundaries, and local government, that is larger than a village and generally smaller than a city.

**Example**: She grew up in a small town in the countryside.

**train**: a series of railroad cars moved as a unit by a locomotive or by integral motors.

**Example**: She took the train to visit her relatives in another state.

**travel**: to go from one place to another, typically over a distance or a journey.

**Example**: She loves to travel to different countries and experience new cultures.

**tree**: a woody perennial plant, typically having a single stem or trunk growing to a considerable height and bearing lateral branches at some distance from the ground.

**Example**: She climbed the tree to retrieve her frisbee that got stuck.

**true**: in accordance with fact or reality; accurate or exact.

**Example**: She spoke the truth when she told her friend what happened.

**try**: make an attempt or effort to do something.

**Example**: She is going to try her best to pass the exam.

**turn**: move in a circular direction wholly or partly around an axis or point.
**Example**: She took a left turn at the traffic lights.

**two**: equivalent to the sum of one and one.

**Example**: She has two younger siblings.

**under**: extending or directly below.

Example: She found her lost keys under the couch.

**until**: up to the point in time or the event mentioned.

**Example:** She waited until her friend arrived before going to the movie theater.

**up**: towards a higher place or position, especially towards the sky.

**Example**: She looked up at the stars.

**us**: used by the speaker or writer to refer to himself or herself and one or more other people as the object of a verb or preposition.

**Example**: She and her friends went on a road trip together and took pictures of us.

**use**: take, hold, or deploy (something) as a means of accomplishing or achieving something.

**Example**: She uses her phone to stay connected with her family and friends.

**usual**: what is ordinarily or generally expected or experienced; normal or customary.

**Example**: She went about her usual daily routine.

**very**: used to emphasize the exactness of a description or the truth of a statement.

**Example**: She was very happy to see her best friend again.

**voice**: the sound produced in a person's larynx and uttered through the mouth, as speech or song.

**Example**: She spoke in a soft and gentle voice.

**wait**: stay where one is or delay action until a particular time or until something else happens.

**Example**: She had to wait for her turn to speak during the meeting.

**walk**: move at a regular and fairly slow pace by lifting and setting down each foot in turn, never having both feet off the ground at once.

**Example**: She likes to walk in the park and enjoy the fresh air.

**want**: have a desire to possess or do (something); wish for.

**Example**: She wants to travel to Japan someday.

**warm**: having, showing, or expressing enthusiasm, affection, or kindness.

**Example**: She gave her friend a warm hug when she saw her after a long time.

**was**: past tense of the verb be, used to indicate that something existed or happened in the past.

**Example**: She was happy to see her family during the holiday season.

**wash**: to clean something with water and soap or other cleaning products.

**Example**: She washed the dishes after dinner.

**watch**: to look at something carefully for a period of time, especially to observe something that is happening or to check the time.

**Example**: She likes to watch movies on the weekend.

**water**: a colorless, transparent, odorless liquid that forms the seas, lakes, rivers, and rain and is the basis of the fluids of living organisms.

**Example**: She drinks plenty of water every day to stay hydrated.

**way:** a method, style, or manner of doing something.

**Example**: She prefers to do things her own way.

**we**: used by the speaker or writer to refer to himself or herself and one or more other people as the subject of a verb or preposition.

**Example**: She and her sister went to the mall together, and we had a great time.

**week**: a period of seven days.

**Example**: She has a busy schedule during the work week.

**weight:** a measure of the heaviness of an object.

**Example**: She lifted the weights at the gym to build her muscles.

**well**: in a good or satisfactory way.

**Example**: She did well on her exam and got an A.

**went**: past tense of the verb go, used to indicate movement from one place to another.

**Example**: She went to the store to buy some groceries.

**were**: past tense of the verb be, used to indicate that something existed or happened in the past.

**Example**: She and her friends were happy to see each other at the party.

**west**: the direction towards the point of the horizon where the sun sets.

**Example**: She enjoys watching the sunset in the west.

**what**: asking for information or clarification about something.

**Example**: She asked her teacher what the homework assignment was.

**wheel**: a circular object that rotates on an axle and is used to facilitate movement or transportation.

**Example**: She rode her bike with the help of its wheels.

**when**: used to introduce a question about the time at which something happened or will happen.

**Example**: She asked her friend when they should meet for lunch.

**where**: used to ask about the location or place of something.

**Example**: She asked her friend where they should go for their next vacation.

**which**: used to introduce a choice between two or more things or to refer to a thing previously mentioned.

**Example**: She wasn't sure which dress to wear to the party.

**while**: a period of time during which something happens.

**Example**: She likes to listen to music while she's doing her homework.

**white**: of the color of milk or fresh snow, due to the reflection of all visible rays of light.

**Example**: She likes to wear a white dress to summer parties.

**who**: used to refer to a person or people as the subject of a verb or as the object of a verb or preposition.

**Example**: She wondered who was going to be at the party.

**whole**: complete; not divided or broken.

**Example**: She ate the whole pizza by herself.

**why**: asking for a reason or explanation.

**Example**: She asked her teacher why she got a low grade on her paper.

**wild**: living or growing in the natural environment; not domesticated or cultivated.

**Example**: She enjoys hiking in the wild outdoors.

**will**: expressing future tense or intention to do something.

**Example**: She will finish her project by the end of the week.

**wind**: a natural movement of air, especially in the form of a current of air blowing from a particular direction.

**Example**: She went kite flying on a windy day.

**winter**: the coldest season of the year, in the northern hemisphere from December to February and in the southern hemisphere from June to August.

**Example**: She likes to go skiing in the winter.

**with**: accompanied by; in the company of.

**Example**: She likes to go to the movies with her friends.

**without:** not having or including; free from.

Example: She went on vacation without her phone.

**wonder:** a feeling of surprise and admiration caused by something beautiful, unexpected, or inexplicable.

**Example:** She wonders about the mysteries of the universe.

**wood:** the hard fibrous material that forms the main substance of a tree or shrub.

**Example:** She likes to use wood to build furniture.

**word:** a single distinct meaningful element of speech or writing, used to form sentences.

**Example:** She carefully chose her words when giving her presentation.

**work:** activity involving mental or physical effort done in order to achieve a purpose or result.

**Example:** She enjoys her work as a teacher.

**world:** the earth, together with all of its countries, peoples, and natural features.

**Example:** She dreams of traveling the world someday.

**would:** used to indicate the consequence of an imagined event or situation.

**Example:** She would be so happy if she won the lottery.

**write:** mark (letters, words, or other symbols) on a surface, typically paper, with a pen, pencil, or similar implement.

**Example:** She likes to write poems in her journal.

**year:** a period of 365 or 366 days, starting from January 1st and ending on December 31st (or on December 30th or 31st if it's a leap year).

**Example:** She is looking forward to the new year's celebrations.

**yes:** used to give an affirmative response.

**Example:** She said yes to his proposal.

**yet:** up until the present or a specified or implied time; still.

**Example:** She hasn't finished her work yet.

**you:** used to refer to the person or people being addressed.

**Example:** She asked How are you? to her friend.

**young:** having lived or existed for only a short time; not old.

**Example:** She enjoys spending time with young children.

**Your:** belonging to or associated with the person or people being addressed.

**Example:** She said Your dress is beautiful to her friend.

# Congratulations!

You did it! 77 Dialogues using the 500 most common words in English. I'm proud of you. It is not easy, but you stuck with it!

I encourage you to go back through the book again. Role play, practice these conversations out loud with friends or fellow classmates.

I believe that repetition is a key to success. The more times you come in contact with certain words and phrases, the more that they will become second nature to you. Don't forget to write some notes in the blank pages that follow.

**If you enjoyed this book, please write me a review. I would love your feedback.**

**Don't forget to find me on social media:**

**Instagram** @camillehanson

**Tiktok** @learnenglishwithcamille

**Youtube** @learnenglishwithcamille

---

# NOTES

Made in United States
Orlando, FL
04 March 2025

59168114R00079